REMEMBER,
I LOVE YOU DEARLY

REMEMBER, I LOVE YOU DEARLY

JOICE "OWL WOMAN"
&
VERNA PERKINS

Spirit Talks Publishing
St. Louis, Missouri

Joice "Owl Woman"/Verna Perkins
Spirit Talks Publishing
P.O. Box 16462
St. Louis, Missouri 63125
www.bandwagonpsychicfair.com

Cover art by: Rhonda Gawedzinski
            Psyrhonda@yahoo.com

Bradford Smith - www.bradfordsmithmusic.com

Richard Novosak - Crystalwisdom@altavista.com

Printed 2000 by: Minuteman Press
                      O'Fallon, Missouri
Second Printing 2002:
                      Publication Printing Co., Inc.
                      2945 Washington Avenue
                      St. Louis, Missouri 63103

ISBN 0-9701246-0-0

U.S. $15.00

ACKNOWLEDGEMENTS

Our special thanks to:

George Greene, psychic and teacher.

Nicholas Tungate, seer and teacher.

The meditation group.

The families of Joice and Verna for their support and love.

Our good friends in the Bandwagon family of psychics, healers and vendors.

PREFACE

References in this book are true accounts of actual events. Names and locations have been changed as necessary.

It is the intent of the authors to inform and educate the reader as he travels through the world of metaphysics.

CHAPTER ONE

i knocked on the door and there was no answer. i went in and, oh, my god, i already knew...i walked into the bedroom...it was too late. she lay across the bed, eyes open...no, please...i hear screaming, screaming!!

I don't even know where to begin any more. I suppose the best thing to do is to go back to the day I met Samantha. I went to a psychic fair with Gregory, Professor of Philosophy at our alma mater, Iowa State University. He is totally into metaphysics, the study relating to a reality beyond what is perceptible to the senses.

Greg has been my best friend since grade school and I confide in him and trust him in nearly everything relating to my work and my personal life. I guess I thought he was crazy to bring me to a place like this, or maybe I thought I was crazy for agreeing to open my life to a total stranger - a psychic, of all things. In truth, I hit a wall with a personal problem, and for a licensed psychologist, that is a ridiculous thing to admit.

"Greg, I feel out of place here. What if one of my patients is here in this room doing the same thing we're doing? What in the hell could I say to defend myself? I'm supposed to have all the answers."

"Look, I come to these things all the time. Remarkable energy is in this room. Tell me you can't feel it in the air."

1

"I don't feel anything, my man. I don't even know what I'm supposed to do."

"Well, all you have to do is walk around the room, pass by each table and observe."

"Observe what?"

"Just watch how the psychics relate to their customers, how they handle the cards and their body language. You can walk the room as many times as you have to until you stop and think, *'this is the one I want to talk with'.* "

"Come on, you have to be joking. They look like anyone on the street. None of them look special...you know, weird."

"You expected to see Gypsies? Come on."

We walked the room, inhaling fragrant incense and getting caught up in the hypnotic Indian recordings. I glanced quickly from face to face - slowing somewhat to catch a word, a phrase, or a clue as to which reader would be the one. Twice around the room, three times, and then - I stopped.

"Greg, I think *she* is the one. She doesn't even use cards."

"Go for it. I'm going down the hall for a lecture on hypnotherapy. I use that technique all the time. One of these days, I'll try it on you!"

He smiled mischievously as he turned away and headed for the door. I felt remarkably at ease as I pulled out the plain metal folding chair and sat to face the table of a woman I would come to know as Samantha. She had loosely curled shoulder-length hair, the color of mahogany. There were fine lines at the corners of her green-blue eyes as she smiled and extended her hand to welcome me into

2

her world. I guessed her to be close to my 46 years, or perhaps a few years younger, and she was dressed rather conservatively except for the unusual feather and crystal jewelry. Unusual from my standpoint, at least. For some reason, I felt an immediate kinship with this woman that I didn't quite understand. Impossible, I thought. This is all part of the game. I went to school for too many years to be sucked into believing anyone could pull information out of thin air.

"My name is Samantha. Will you please sign in?" I took the pen and wrote my name below at least twenty others.

hmm, lucrative little business here!

At first I was tempted to make up a different name, but I didn't. I scribbled, *William*, in my usual, illegible hand.

She turned the notebook slightly, read my name, and said, "William, the charge is $25 and $5 more if you want a tape recording of this reading."

I reached for my wallet and produced the $30. I definitely wanted Greg to hear this! I had removed my wedding ring in the lobby of the hotel before we came into the room and slipped it into my pocket along with my Rolex. My khaki pants and buttoned-down blue dress shirt would not give away any information about my profession.

Samantha pressed the recorder to the "on" position and took my hands in hers. I knew my hands would be cool, because for some reason, they are always cool. She said nothing about my hands at all. In fact, she said nothing. Her eyes were closed.

that's effective!

3

"William? Do they call you William?"

"Yes. I was thinking about putting down a fictitious name, but I changed my mind. I wanted to trick you, because in truth, I am a bit skeptical."

"I would have picked up on that. In fact, you *do* have an imagination, but along with that imagination is a vision and a practicality to put that imagination to good use. You are beneficial to others. You love people and you give help whenever needed. You restore harmony and order in very individual ways. People respect you because they realize you are fair and can be trusted.

"I see that in some circumstances you can be inflexible, almost to the point of being stubborn, and that causes you problems. I see you coming on strong but there is another side of you that is cautious. You have impatience with people who act irrationally because you want the best for them in life. I see extreme honesty. I also see that you have difficulty talking about something that hurts you.

"You are taking way too much responsibility in a relationship; you put up with too much. Are you a married man?"

"Yes."

"There is a difficulty there. I see two children."

"No, I only have one."

"I am getting two children. Is your child a boy?"

"Yes, but he is twenty-seven and has a son of his own. My grandson, Nicholas, is six."

"You're taking over quite a lot of your wife's responsibility in the home and possibly socially, right now. I don't see the situation improving for some time, possibly as long as 6 months or more. Is your wife ill? I see a disturbance of some kind in the energy field; there could be a hospitalization, but only for a short period of time. Does your wife suffer from high blood pressure?"

"I don't know."

"It would be a good thing to have it checked. You can be a little stubborn at times but you should not question this suggestion for your wife.

"I feel that you have a charming curiosity. You put other people at ease and you get them to reveal themselves to you. You want to know everything about everything. I see a spiritual quality in you that will bring out the response of others. This is the inner self of your personality and it feels as if you have help. Like a cosmic helper. What is your occupation?"

"I am a psychologist."

"Do you ever work with children?"

"Some of the patients referred to me are children, but not a lot."

"I see a child behind you as you sit with me. The child has a connection with you and you will become aware of him. Does the name James mean anything to you?"

"I know a lot of people named James. Oh, my grandson's middle name is James."

"This will be someone you will connect with spiritually.

"I feel you are seeking answers to the point of becoming jittery, and your enormous amount of energy needs to be focused. Perhaps you are seeking answers in the wrong places. The answers are inside of you and you must pay more attention. Your own inner wisdom is wiser for you than any book, any teacher, or any minister - when you listen to it. You are coming to a clearing - if you remain quiet and ask."

"I don't understand; who should I ask? "

"God. Just sit quietly and ask. We have a higher self that I always think of as the Christ within us. Ask that it be revealed to you and watch what happens. It is time for you to be nicer to yourself, relax, meditate, put your problems into small spaces and deal with them one by one.

"You may ask any questions you wish."

Samantha released my hands and watched me. I'm sure she saw that I was bewildered.

"Oh, I didn't know I could ask anything," I stammered. "I guess I'd have to say first that I am totally surprised at how much you know about me. How do you do it?"

"I do not make assumptions about you. I have a spirit guide. I am giving you only the information I am receiving. And, when the information stops, there is no more and it's your turn to ask questions. My guide will tell us what the answers will be."

"Well, this is tough for me to ask. My wife...she has this drinking problem and I don't know what I can do to make her stop. Can you help me at all with that?"

"What is her name and her age, and where is she now?"

"Julia. She's a few months younger than I am, 46, and she's a teacher. I think she would be at home now - at our house - this being Saturday, and all. I came here on my own with a friend."

Samantha turned her head away from me for a moment and dropped her gaze toward the floor. Then she focused her attention back to me, but did not take my hands.

"She is clearly troubled and I feel that you have worn yourself thin with your effort to help her. She does not want any help; she will stop when she is ready; she is not ready at this time."

"How much time are we talking here? I am going crazy with my work, taking care of the house, the shopping, checking on Julia continually to make sure she doesn't do anything foolish. And sometimes, on weekends, my son asks us to baby sit Nicholas, but I have not been able to tell him the truth about his mother. I just say OK, and then I have to figure out how to do that, too. I am a psychologist, for God's sake, and I can't even get through to my own wife! Do you know how that makes me feel?"

Samantha was silent.

Then, "You must take care of yourself. I see your family as a source of help with this. You must ask for help at least until Julia starts to heal. Your son is an adult. He will be all right with this. He will not be happy, but he will be all right. This may take some time."

She was silent again.

"Stop and think before you demand that she stop drinking. Allow yourself quiet time to get in touch with your inner soul. I see the strength you have. You have insight far greater than you realize. You have the ability to see things coming that others do not see. You will be developing that gift. You will use that gift to help others. You have great things to accomplish and you have the power to do so. Do not underestimate yourself. Are there any other questions?"

"That was my only question, really, and my only reason for coming here today. I asked Greg to take me with him when he came for a reading and that's why I'm here with you. You have given me good information; I know that."

Samantha smiled. "It was very nice to have met you today, and please take one of my cards with you."

"Thanks, I will."

I reached to the cardholder. Her first name was inscribed, but not her last name, and other things were listed.

...past-life regression, hypnotherapy.

"How long you have been doing this work? It amazes me! I've never met anyone like you."

"Everyone in this room does what I do. I was given this gift when I was eight years old and this is how I make my living. I travel all over the United States helping people just like you do, except that I can reach them on a higher level. I see your potential in that respect also. It has always been there. You should not ignore the power within you."

She smiled at me again, ejected my recorded cassette, and passed it to me across the table. I had a strong feeling that I needed to stay longer, to hear more, but as I shifted my weight to leave the chair, I noticed two more names beneath mine on her notebook. She had kept my attention to the point of thinking no one else was in the room, except the two of us.

...and one exceptionally generous guide.

I nearly jumped out of my skin - Greg was sitting on a chair behind me, within a few feet of Samantha's table.

"Greg! You startled me! Did you hear anything she told me?"

"No," he replied, with a smile. "How did it go?"

"You won't believe it. I can hardly believe it, myself. Can we play this tape on the way back? You have to hear all the things she told me."

I stopped and said, "Oh, I'm sorry. Are you ready to go or do you want to get a reading? Or, maybe you want to go to another class, or buy something?"

"I'm ready if you are. Want to stop for a burger?"

"Yah, fine, but I want to run this tape for you. Let's drive around for a while before we eat. I'm really excited about this! She gave me some help with Julia and she said some things about me that I suspected for a long time. Wait till you hear it! You know how I say things, and then later it happens? Well, get this...she picked up on that, too."

"Doesn't surprise me in the least. I always knew you were goofy! Don't look at me like that. I'm kidding!"

We punched each other as we headed for the door, and we laughed like children who had just gotten away with something. We ran the length of the parking lot and piled into Gregory's white custom van. I took the opportunity once again to berate him on his choice of country western music as I ejected his tape and pushed in my cassette. Anyone looking through the side windows as we drove west would have thought I was out of my mind. I was literally bouncing in my seat.

"Listen to that! Lets run it back; wait a minute, what did she say? Holy cow, she got me. I have to improve on that one. Do I really seem that way to you?"

Lunch was as upbeat as our review of the tape. I asked Gregory a lot of questions about his psychic experiences and about his study of metaphysics. He answered all of them. Then, on the drive home from the restaurant, he suggested I come to his house the following Wednesday evening to sit in on meditation with a group of friends. He said it would open my mind to another dimension of thought, and it would give me a night free from my frustration with Julia. I agreed to the plan and told him I was excited about learning how to meditate.

Greg dropped me off about 3:00 p.m. and I entered to face Julia with a refreshed outlook on our future. It was quiet, and the shades were drawn. I found her in front of the television in the living room, a bottle of vodka wedged between the sofa arm and her left thigh. She did not acknowledge me.

My usual reaction to this was to raise my voice until she responded, which would start an angry flurry of accusations. I felt more empowered and decided to try to accept the fact that I could not change anything. I walked to her side and kissed her gently on the side of her head, slightly brushing her straight blonde hair with my lips. Maybe I expected a reaction, I don't know. There was nothing.

Sunday was a re-run of every other Sunday with Julia. She slept until noon, headed blindly for the coffeepot and a cigarette and padded back into her bedroom. She chose to sleep in a room separate from mine. I missed her. I wished life could return to the way it was, but I had to shoot for life with changes for the better. It eluded me how she managed to function during the week as a teacher and come home to smoke and drink until she passed out. She was thin and she'd become sloppy in her choice of loose-fitting clothing after having been a stylish dresser. Her light hair was graying, as was mine, but I wished she would consider having it styled rather than string-straight and parted with red barrettes.

I started dinner and put laundry in the washer. Julia was generally incapable of functioning around the house and now refused to pick up her clothes as well, so I resented laundry duty even more. I thought about leaving her things lay on the floor until she totally ran out of underwear, but I couldn't do that to her. I knew I had to be patient and understanding even though it was becoming increasingly difficult. I felt myself slipping into the same depression I found manifested in my patients. I decided to speak to my son and daughter-in-law. Samantha told me I would get support from them.

Dinnertime came and went. Julia did not come to the kitchen. I didn't know when or what she ate any more. She did her usual trick of passing out on the couch and at 11:00 I went into my room and closed the door. She usually managed to get to her room, sleep it off and get to work on time the next morning. How many years could this go on before her body broke down? Her spirit left her long ago.

CHAPTER TWO

My office hours started mid-afternoon and ran until eight o'clock in the evening so that I could see people after they left work. I sometimes blamed myself for Julia's drinking problem.

if i were at home with her more, things would be different.

But, I felt that Samantha's reading was on track and it was up to Julia to make a decision. Her visits to AA were unsuccessful the previous year. She simply did not want to stop drinking.

I decided to change my schedule to attend Greg's Wednesday meditation, and my secretary handled it well. My last consultation would end by 6:30 p.m. on that day so I could get to Greg's on time.

Then it was Wednesday night and I was late. Peter Lee was upset with his supervisor, his wife and his car. I had a difficult time getting him to understand my suggestions for the following week. Finally, I got my jacket and his jacket and we left the office together. When I walked up the steps to Greg's porch, I realized I remembered nothing of the drive. My mind was on Samantha and I wondered if it was foolish to think *getting in touch with my inner soul* would make any sense to my scientifically structured mind. Greg opened the door and greeted me with a smile, a handshake and of all things, a bear hug.

"You made it! Come on in!"

I was surprised at the number of people in the room. They ranged in age from about twenty to sixty-five, male and female.

"This is my friend, William," Greg said proudly. "We have been friends since we were children and he knows more about me than I care to reveal."

I grinned and nodded to everyone and with that, each of the guests approached and embraced me.

what's with this?

Greg saw the look on my face and laughed.

"Hey, they do this all the time!"

There was a chair for me between a heavy-set man named Rodney and a girl named Marie, who was close to my son's age. Greg lit several vanilla candles in the room and asked Marilyn (30-ish) to turn off the light next to her.

i guess we're starting.

We were instructed by Greg to stand, hold hands, and form a circle of healing. He asked that we close our eyes and follow along with him:

"We are surrounded in the pure white light of God. Only good will come to us; only good will go from us."

Then Greg said, "Picture energy in the form of white light coming down into your crown chakra. Now, add your own energy and send it out of your right hand to the next person."

The energy formed an unbroken chain and was contained within the circle. One by one, each guest suggested someone to be placed in the healing circle, and each gave a short description of the pain or illness being suffered by that individual. Greg said we were to picture the person, isolate the area of pain in our minds and send collective healing energy to that spot in the form of a white light. The entire time we were to concentrate only on the specific task set before us. I was moved by the intensity of the scene.

When it was my turn, I said, "I'd like to put my wife, Julia, into the circle. She is 46 years old and has been suffering from alcoholism for several years. She is at home now, probably in the living room on our blue couch."

Greg said, "Let's all picture Julia. Bring a bright, white light over the top of her head, down over her crown chakra, over her shoulders, down around her arms and solar plexus, over her abdomen, over her hips, down her legs and wrap it around and under her feet. Let us hold it there for a few minutes. She is feeling the healing energy. Now, picture in your mind a shower of pink hearts floating down around her."

I held my eyes tightly closed and tears began to roll from the corners. We were silent.

And then Greg said, "Next."

We spent sufficient time with each healing and returned quietly to our seats.

i feel so good about this...i wish i knew whether or not julia can feel something...these are good people.

It was quiet in the room. Everyone seemed at peace. Greg moved to his tape deck and inserted a cassette. He returned to his place and asked us to sit comfortably, close our eyes and place palms up on our laps to "receive."

receive? receive what?

The recording was *New Dance*, original music composed for the Native American Lacota Indian flute by Bradford Smith. Greg told us he was going to suggest a relaxing technique. We were to concentrate on his voice until we had entered into a totally relaxed state. At that

14

time, we would be open to receive messages from our guides.

ok. i can do this.

"Relax your body completely and imagine yourself at the seashore. See the waves washing onto the white sand. You are walking along the beach and you see footprints taking you back in time, seeking the level you need to achieve to do your work tonight. For those of you who are here for the first time, create a place that is peaceful and quiet. Get to know the entire area, inside and outside, so that you can return to this place each time. Your guide will meet you there. For the rest of you, enjoy your journey and I will count you back up when it is time to return."

i see nothing but blackness. now i see a little light coming in. i'll picture myself under a large oak tree. it is summer and the tree is bountiful. the tree is in a grassy area in the middle of nothing, and i'm sitting there, holding my knees, looking around. i'm putting in an ocean now and it is many colors of blue. now it's dark. it's as if someone has pulled a black screen in front of my eyes. i see the outline of a face. it's the profile of a man. it scares me. i don't know what to do. the profile is drifting slowly toward me and now it is moving off to the right and out of my vision. i want it to stay and turn and look at me; i want to see who it is, but I can't. it's dark again. i see another profile coming toward me and it appears to be the face of a woman. it's moving closer to me and now it is starting to drift to the side. please turn toward me so i can see who you are. i want to see your face. you won't turn. i want more, but there is no more. there's only blackness. i can hear greg telling us to come back...

"I'm going to ask you to start coming back now," said Greg, softly. "Say good-by to your guides and begin to return slowly. You will remember what you saw and what you heard. I will begin to count backward from five. ...5, 4, 3, 2, 1. You are coming back now, and you are feeling awake and alert."

i don't think i want to wake up yet. i'm in such a state of relaxation. why was there no guide in my meditation? a guide could have helped me; a guide could have given me answers.

We had been meditating for about fifteen minutes. I opened my eyes and the other guests were moving around in their chairs, trying to get back to reality. I realized that two of the women had moved to the floor with couch pillows during their meditation. Greg looked as if he had been down with us. His eyes looked very tired. Several people left the room to get drinks or use the bathroom. Two people went out on the porch to smoke. I could not move. I was mesmerized. This was old stuff to them; this was monumental for me. What in the world was going on in my subconscious? Who were those faces in my mind? Did I do what everyone else did?

Greg was bombarded with questions almost immediately, and when he was free, he walked over to my chair.

"Well, how did you do?"

"I can't believe it, Greg. I actually saw some stuff!"

"Great! Some people come here and don't see anything for weeks. When everybody gets back from a break, we'll take turns telling what we saw." And he was off to get a soda in the kitchen. I followed him.

"Greg, where's Sandra? Doesn't she do this with you?"

"No. There are some couples with the same psychic interests, but nobody here tonight is a *couple*. "

"Really? That surprises me."

"It is pretty consistent. One of the two is interested and the other is scoffing or worse yet, condemning. We walk in the light, not the darkness, and we are free to make choices. There may be an older couple of retirement age who go everywhere together, so they try this. And there are some people who are hoping to eventually meet a *significant other* who will be a partner in healing. You put Julia in the healing circle tonight. It was a good thing to do."

"It was wonderful, Greg. I had no idea. The group is strong and I feel very good about being a part of it. Each person is sincere; each person has someone he wants to help. How did you form this group?"

"I don't really know. They all sort of fell in the door, one by one. Someone knew someone who had been here before, or someone brought a friend who knew he had something special. All of them have had premonitions or have had coincidences that could not otherwise be explained. They all feel things that others cannot. They have the gift and they want to share it and help people. Some are stronger than others. You should come back often - heck, come back every week!"

"I'll consider it, Greg. If nothing else, I want to strengthen myself and then try to help Julia. I want to learn alternatives because my psychology is out the window. Nothing I say makes a difference. You heard the tape. Samantha is right. And deep inside, I know it too. Julia has to make the decision to stop; she has to decide when that will be."

"And she will. I'll support you in any way I can, William. You can call me at home or at work any time."

"Thanks."

"I see the group is back. Let's go share our meditations with them. I'm particularly interested in yours."

The stories were beyond anything I'd imagined. There were bears, wolves and Indians who acted as guides and gave answers to their questions.

i'll have to ask greg why i didn't see a guide. i guess i'm not ready for that.

Some traveled to far-away lands; others saw themselves on ships at sea. One woman walked with the spirit of an angel, describing the white wings that wrapped around her, leaving her warm and secure. A young girl saw a horse running along side of her, and I had the urge to tell her that a deer was going to run in front of her car.

just because i think about it doesn't mean it will happen. i can't tell her such a thing.

The older gentleman, Larry, said that his guide was a young boy who always appeared and showed him things. The things he showed did not make sense to Larry and we all tried to give them meaning. He looked bewildered and stopped his story abruptly, frustrated that it was nothing he could understand.

wait until it's my turn. no one will be able to interpret mine, either.

Then it *was* my turn. I was so excited and everyone was astonished that I got something on the first try. They loved my profile images! One of the men suggested the female image might have indicated Julia, who cannot face me. Now that was reaching just a bit. Julia was alive and well and couldn't possibly be showing up in my meditations.

or, does it mean that the spirits are aware and are showing me it is understood? i wonder if we interpret our subconscious thoughts in the direction we choose?

When all the stories had been shared, the group broke up and stood in the center of the room for another few minutes of sharing with each other. In some cases, there were words of encouragement for relatives and friends who had been put into the healing circle. In other cases, it was a friendly hug and a wish for a good week. Everyone I spoke to encouraged me to return again as soon as my schedule would allow.

I hung around until everyone had gone and thanked Greg for inviting me. He reassured me that what we learn through meditation has meaning just for the individual and sometimes it is not clear. He said our life path is pre-set at birth and hinges on our past lives.

"I'm not going to begin to ask you about that statement. I'll call you soon. I have to go home and check on Julia. I hope she felt something positive tonight."

"She did, but she didn't recognize it for what it was. We have a lot of work to do together and she'll come around in time. Call me when you need to talk about it."

I don't live far from Greg's house, and I was home in less than ten minutes. The lights were out and Julia had gone to bed. She didn't even care to know that I was all right. It would never have crossed her mind to worry about me. Nothing ever got through to her when she was drinking.

CHAPTER THREE

I didn't have to be a brain surgeon to know I was trapped in a new adventure. It felt like an awakening. I ran Samantha's tape again later in the week and heard things I hadn't heard before. At least they had not registered. I wondered about Julia's blood pressure and how I could get her in for a check-up. There would be no way she'd agree to see a doctor. I tried to meditate on my own one night after I went to bed, but when I relaxed, I fell asleep. I tried to meditate in the office during my lunch hour, but I saw nothing.

Greg called and left a message that he had several books on metaphysical study he thought I would be interested in reading. He said he would drop them off with my secretary. I called him back the next day and told him I could cancel my Wednesday evening appointments again in a few weeks, and I could get the books that night at his class. He was delighted.

My visits to meditation classes became more frequent and I was feeling very good about my progress. Greg led us in psychic awareness games with objects and notes in sealed envelopes, and I watched in astonishment one night when he showed his mastery of the Ouija board.

"Greg, do you remember when we played with the board when we were growing up?" I asked. "We could never get it to work."

"Yah, and I remember you heard the Ouija was a bad thing to have in your house, so for some reason, you put it in the freezer!"

"I didn't know how I was supposed to get rid of it without it bringing some kind of bad luck. I probably should have burned it. My Mom ended up giving it away. So does this one really work?"

"They all work," laughed Scott, a young man in the group, who I found out later, was hooked on the investigation of UFO's.

"You have to know what you're doing. You can't just *play* with the board unless you want to have a bad experience."

Scott sat down in front of Greg and said, "I'll be Greg's partner and call out the letters for him. Will you write everything down, William?"

"Sure," I said, still harboring disbelief.

maybe there's something to this, but i don't know anybody who could ever get a message from one of these.

I soon discovered that it was not a parlor game. Greg was adamant about that. Everyone in the room had to follow along with him in this preparatory statement for his own protection as well as ours:

"We are surrounded in the pure white light of God. Only good will come to us; only good will go from us.

"We are surrounded by four gold bands - one around our ankles, one around our waist, one around our head and one that arches above us and circles below us. We want to call in only high guides who walk in the light."

Scott placed the board on a footstool in front of Gregory and took his place on the floor, opposite the board. Greg and Scott put their fingertips lightly on the plastic planchette and it began to rotate slowly over the surface of the Ouija board. Slowly, slowly...

Suddenly the planchette took off like a shot. It stopped on a letter and Scott yelled,
"M!"
The planchette moved and stopped at the left.
"A!"
Greg's hands moved quickly to the right.
"N!"
And then to the far right...
"Y!"
I was writing the letters as fast as I could. Scott was up on his knees trying to keep a close eye on the letters as the planchette flew from one to the other. When it stopped, I looked at my paper. I had literally scribbled,
MANY CHOICES MUCH GROWTH IN CHOICES
No time to think; their hands were flying again.
Scott called out, "M! A! R! I! E! D! R! I! N! K! M! O! R! E! W! A! T! E! R!
Their hands hesitated and stopped. Greg's eyes looked strange. He looked like he was far away...somewhere else.
he doesn't watch the board; he's not picking out the letters. i love this guy!
I looked down at my paper.
"Holy cow! Someone go get Marie off the porch. There's a message here for her."
I flipped to a fresh page in the notebook and got ready. Their hands started moving in a slow circle and, wham! They were off again.
Scott yelled, "W! I! L! E! Y! E! S! O! P! E! N! G! O! O! D! W! O! R! K! S!
Their hand stopped. I looked at the paper.

22

no way! this is for me!
Greg and Scott gave me no time to digest the message. Scott was calling letters. We worked a little while longer until suddenly, their hands stopped. There were three more messages for people in the room and I got up and handed them out. Greg looked drained. He fell back in the chair and Scott sat down on the floor, equally exhausted.

"What did I tell you William?" Scott asked. "Are you impressed yet?"

"I can't stand it. This is the craziest thing I have ever seen. Where do these messages come from? Greg, you weren't even looking at the board!"

"Our guides come through and give us the messages," Greg replied. "Our hands move automatically. We have no control of the messages or where our hands move. It's pretty amazing stuff, isn't it?"

"Do you ever remember the words you get?"

"No, we never know what came through us. Our group enjoys the evenings we work with the Ouija board because they look forward to receiving messages. Nothing surprises them any more."

"Well it's new to me. I can't believe you got six messages. And one of them was mine. It says, *Wil - eyes - open - good - works.* I'm not exactly sure what it means, but I guess it has something to do with studying here with your group. I passed out the other messages so they can tell you what they got."

"That's all right, but I don't think they will. They have meaning only for the person who receives. Not everyone in the room gets a message each time. You were lucky."

23

"Do you think I can learn to do the board, Greg?"

"I think in time you may be able to do it if you practice often with a compatible partner."

"I'm open to learn everything. Do you think it's good that I can feel when a certain thing is going to happen?"

"William, you get messages all the time. You should pay more attention to them; be more aware of what you're being shown."

Rodney overheard our conversation and came over to us with his piece of paper and the message I wrote. He thanked Greg for receiving it, but did not share the contents. Instead, he looked at me.

"William, I've been wondering if we've been able to give your wife any help since we put her in the healing circle. Have there been any improvements, or have you seen any changes?"

"I wish I could say yes, Rodney, but there haven't been any signs of change. She wants to be left alone. I want to get her to a doctor for a checkup, too. Do you know Samantha? She told me Julia should be checked for high blood pressure."

"Everybody knows Samantha. She has a reputation for being the best. If she told you Julia has a problem, believe me, she has a problem. You definitely need to look into it. I guess you could say I'm here because of something I discovered about my health too, if you can consider stuttering a health problem. It isn't, but it affected my life - every day of my life, from a psychological standpoint. And you know about that, don't you."

"Of course. But then I work with people who have all types of abnormal problems."

"My wife made an appointment for me with Samantha at her home. She took me into a past life where I had a speech defect that caused me to stutter. She taught me how to leave the defect in the past and not bring it forward into the present."

"It must have worked, Rodney. You don't stutter at all."

"Not any more, I don't! Totally unbelievable, isn't it? Samantha worked with me for an hour and a half, and what more can I tell you? All I know is that when I left her house, I no longer stuttered. After that wonderful experience, my wife Barbara and I opened our home and set up an atmosphere for learning. We meet on Sunday evenings about seven and sometimes work together as late as twelve or one o'clock in the morning. Would you like to join us?"

"What do you do? Is there a large group?"

"It varies; it usually averages about eight people. They bring in books and we read together, we study energies through the Ouija board, and we do alternative healing and meditation. We get together for Indian pow-wows and attend psychic fairs in the area. It can be fun and I can guarantee it will be another learning experience for you. Samantha is going to come in one of these Sundays and teach us past-life regression."

"It sounds good, Rodney. I'll see what I can do. Here, write your phone number and address on the back of my Ouija message. Is Samantha's husband interested in the metaphysical field also?"

"No, there is no husband. She's been divorced for ten years."

CHAPTER FOUR

Several weekends later, I did call. Barbara and Rodney, both in their late 50's, were excellent hosts. Barbara would buy special desserts because Rodney loved to snack throughout the evening. Sometimes we would be in serious discussions and he would sneak off to the dining room to cut into a cheesecake before the rest of us realized he was gone. Or, we would be coming out of mediation to the sound of a plastic lid snapping off of the chocolate angelfood cake container.

Beneath the lighthearted facade, the techniques used in this advanced group were far ahead of what I experienced at Greg's. Meditations were a rich source of information, as I was finally able to reach a spirit guide who showed me life beyond my grasp and provided answers to my questions. I was just getting comfortable with my progress when I got really sick and ended up in the hospital.

I can quote Dr. Jordan exactly. When I had his answering service page him on Friday evening to tell him I had a 103.5 degree fever and couldn't keep anything down, he said, "There's something going around."

He said he would call my pharmacy and that I should get in a tub of cool water to break the fever. He left the bad news for last.

"You will be sick as a dog for about five days."

Julia found me in my room Saturday afternoon, burning with fever. Apparently she had slept late as usual, come down for coffee and actually realized I was not around. Thank goodness. When she got no response from me, she called our son Mark and they got me to the emergency room at Mercy Hospital Medical Center in downtown Des Moines.

I was aware of nothing for hours. My fever brought on convulsions and I was dehydrated. Julia and Mark were there when I finally opened my eyes. I didn't know where I was or what time it was, and the room seemed cloudy or something. I remember reaching for the bed rail to try to sit up, but I was attached to an IV board. There were wires stuck on me and I could see monitors just beyond a glass wall.

"What the HELL!" I screamed. "Get this goddamned stuff off me and get me the hell out of here!"

Mark jumped out of his chair; Julia jumped out of her chair.

"Dad, it's OK. You don't have to talk like that. What's wrong with you?"

Julia looked stunned. "William, please, you're embarrassing us."

"Embarrassing YOU? YOU'RE THE DRUNK! YOU'RE the one who should be hog-tied and tube fed!"

"I'm going out for a cigarette," she huffed, and turned for the double doors.

"The HELL YOU ARE! You get your sorry butt over there and watch those monitors! THAT'S your job. You're taking care of ME, bitch!"

An orderly came rushing in. I'll bet he thought he was going to calm me down, but I was too smart for that. I yanked the needle out of my arm and cursed him. He was an ox. He grabbed my shoulders, climbed up on the bed and forced my chest down under both his knees. He was screaming for help. With that, nurses and orderlies came from everywhere, and in a minute, I was strapped down like an animal. I called those idiots every name in the book and pulled with all the strength I had in me until somebody hit me with a needle.

Julia and Mark were ushered to the hall and they stood there, huddled together.

"Mom, what the heck is wrong with him? My father never talked like that in his life. He's like a wild animal!"

"I don't know, Mark. Maybe it's the fever. He's the most mild-mannered man on the planet."

"Until today," Mark moaned. "I sure hope he snaps out of it by the time the medication wears off. It *has* to be the fever. I can't imagine what the people here are thinking. He has a good reputation at this hospital."

"And what will they say about me, Mark? Everyone will know he's married to a *drunk*. And you had to hear it this way. I'm so sorry you were in there. I think I am the cause of all this. He must have snapped. He's been pretty much taking care of everything for a long time and protecting me," Julia said, as she began to sob.

Mark put his arms around his mother and love was in his heart. They stood holding each other for a long time. An orderly came out of the room.

"Maybe the two of you would like to go to the waiting room. He's asleep now and we put him back on fluids. He will be admitted to a room and we'll let you know the room number shortly."

"Thanks," said Mark, and he took Julia's hand.

When Mark drove me home from the hospital on Tuesday, I was not the same William. My mind was jumbled and my body was weak. Julia did her best to help me, but her urge for alcohol was too strong. She succumbed to the demon in the bottle and I was alone.

Mark was the only one I had left to depend on. He was sick over his mother and his father. He told me that while I was tied down in the hospital, I was telling the doctor not to believe anything his no-good wife said because the "bitch is a drunken liar." He said I called *him* "the bastard son of the devil." I don't remember any of it.

I have Mark to thank for saving my practice. He went to my office and had a long, personal talk with my secretary. Between the two of them, they called on a former associate of mine and he agreed to take my patient load until I was well enough to return. I remember thinking I didn't care. It didn't matter to me.

My first week out of the hospital proved to be somewhat of an adventure. Julia stumbled around every morning getting ready for work, and I was content to sit at the kitchen table and watch. She would glare at me and I would smile and continue to sip my coffee. Every morning she would be running late, throwing her things around, squealing the tires as she shot out of the driveway.

I took walks around the block, watched television and generally didn't give a rap. Julia would return at 4:00 in the afternoon and everything was the same as when she left. I had no desire to be a domestic. I chalked it up to bad effects from the fever. Frozen dinners were fine and I found myself a block away at the drive-thru ordering tacos for lunch. I never ate Mexican food before I got sick. I hated Mexican food.

Mark stopped in around 6:30 p.m. on Friday when he got off work. He is a graphic artist at an advertising firm in southeast Des Moines. I was so pleased to see him. My Mark is a mirror image of me at twenty-seven, with his dark brown curly hair and bright blue eyes.

"Dad, how's it going?" he asked, a look of concern on his face.

"Oh, great, Mark. Come on in."

"Wow! What hit this place? Can I help you straighten up?"

"Nah, it's all right. Who the f--- cares."

"Dad, are you sure you are all right? When do you think you can go back to the office? I talked to Pauline and she said the appointments are going along well with Dr. Vargas, but she is concerned that your patients will be looking for you. You know they may feel uneasy about working with a different psychologist."

"Mark, this is hard for me to understand, but my clothes don't even look familiar. I looked in my closet this morning and I saw all those suits and wondered who they belonged to!"

"*WHAT?*"

"And that's not the half of it. I got in my car to go to the grocery store a couple days ago. I knew where I wanted to go, but I didn't know how to get there. I think I'm f---'n crazy. Do you have a road map in your car? I have to have one."

"Oh my God, Dad. What's going on with you? It must be from the fever. It cooked your brain, or something. I knew you were nuts in the hospital - all that filthy talk. Mom and I were horrified. And you're still using the '*f*' word. Do you realize what you're doing? You never talked like that before. I'm really worried about you."

"Well, relax. I'm not worried. I just don't get it. I

30

know you think I should go back to work but you can see why it's impossible. And, I have been seeing things - like not seeing, exactly, but knowing things."

"What kinds of things?" Mark asked, horrified.

"Well, like when the doorbell rang just now, I knew it was you before I opened the door. And earlier today, something told me to call Gregory and he said he was just about to call me. What is that?"

"I don't understand this at all, Dad. What kind of medication are you taking?"

"The doctor didn't give me anything. They pumped me full of antibiotics, the fever came down, and they signed me out. I don't feel bad at all. That's what's strange. No headaches, no dizziness, but I'm totally confused about what I'm supposed to be doing. I just hope it's not early Alzheimers. If something happens to me, your mother won't have anybody."

"Is Mom here? I didn't see her car."

"It's in the garage. Julia's in her room, but you wouldn't want to see her at this hour of the day, trust me. I've been home for four days and she hasn't noticed anything different about me. She is in a world of her own."

"Look, how about if I go pick up a couple of chicken dinners for you and Mom before I head home?"

"Sure, why not. I don't think I'll be able to get your mother to come to the kitchen, but I'll take it in to her."

Mark returned shortly with our dinners and hesitated at the door. I could tell he hated to leave his parents in such a state. But he had a family of his own, and I told him his responsibility was with them. Julia and I would work things out and call if we needed help.

Well, it didn't stop there. Every day was filled with surprises. The chocolate I craved in the past tasted awful. I stopped at a discount store and bought six pair of baggy shorts and a bunch of pocket T-shirts. The colors did not matter, or the plaids, or whether or not they matched. I couldn't find any tennis shoes in my closet, so they were put on my shopping list. And white socks. Comfort was the name of the game. I actually decided that Julia made a decent salary, so why should I work?

And then on a Tuesday afternoon I got a phone call. It was Rodney.

"William? Gregory called and told me you were in the hospital. It was the flu or something, wasn't it?"

"You could say that," I laughingly replied.

"Sunday," said Rodney, "Samantha is coming in to teach us past-life regression. We are all pretty excited about it and thought, if you feel up to it, you might like to join us."

"Rodney, I'm so glad you called. I'm a mess. I don't understand why everything is different in my life. I don't know what's happening to me."

I gave him my story in a nutshell. He wasn't surprised for some reason. He said there were answers for me, all right, but not the answers I would expect to hear. I agreed to join him and his group on Sunday. Any solution would satisfy me at this point in time.

CHAPTER FIVE

I was excited to be back on familiar ground when I drove up to Rodney's house five days later. And the best part was the fact that I remembered where he lived. Rodney greeted me at the door clutching two glazed donuts. I had to laugh.

"William! I'm so glad you made it. Guess who's here?"

"Samantha?"

"Yes, of course she's here, but I invited your buddy, Gregory. I thought he would be a good partner for you in the regression."

I felt more secure knowing I would be in good hands. I could see Greg chatting with Samantha in the far corner of the living room, so I walked directly over to join them.

Greg stood.

"Aren't you surprised to see me, William? How are you feeling?"

He put his arm around my shoulder.

"Physically, I'm fine, but my head is still not on straight. It sure is good to see you, Greg."

"You remember Samantha, don't you?"

"Of course."

Samantha gave me what I thought looked like a blank stare.

"Did we meet?" she asked, as I reached over to take her hand.

"Sure! I'm William. Remember, you did my first

reading at the Embassy Suites about two months ago."

"Oh, forgive me."

She smiled and stood to acknowledge me.

"When I give readings, I'm on a different level. The messages are not for me and I forget them as soon as I relay them. I don't remember the client unless he comes to me regularly."

"Samantha, I have so many questions. I can't begin to tell you what's been happening to me. I hope you can give me some time after class. Or, maybe I can set up a consultation with you on another day. I know you can help me sort out some things."

"I *do* see clients at my home, William. I think you may need more than a few one-liners. We'll set up an appointment after class tonight, all right?"

"That would be excellent," I agreed, eagerly.

I took a chair opposite them as Rodney stepped to the center of the room to start the class.

"If anyone wants more donuts, he will have to wait until later. I would like Samantha to start us on past-life regressions now, because it will take quite a bit of time. Samantha, it's all yours."

Samantha asked for introductions around the room and then led the group toward the hallway. She told us to choose a partner for the exercise, and Greg was my man.

We were asked to enter separate rooms with our partners and Samantha came to work with us first.

"Gregory? William? Which one of you would like to regress the other?"

Greg gave me a silly grin and said, "I'm the one with all the experience. I'll regress William."

Samantha asked, "Do you know how to take him

down and move him back in time?"

"Of course. My hypnotherapy expertise will come in handy. Remember William, I told you I would hypnotize you some day!"

Samantha nodded in agreement at the choice and said, "Please begin. I'll go to help the others and come back to check on your progress."

As Greg counted and moved me back, I could feel myself dropping down to another level.

Greg said, "You will either see something, hear something or feel something. And perhaps it will be a combination of all of those things."

"All right, William, is it day or night?"

"Day."

"Are you in the country or city?"

"Country."

"Look at your feet; what kind of shoes are you wearing?"

"None."

"Look at the rest of your clothing. What are you wearing?"

"Buckskin...Indian buckskin."

"Do you know where you are?"

"In the mountains."

"Do you know the year?"

"No."

"Do you have a family?"

"Yes."

"Do you have a wife?"

"Yes."

"Do you have children?"

"Yes."

"When we start bringing in other people, look in their eyes. You will be able to tell if they are people from this lifetime. The eyes are the windows to the soul.

"Where is your wife?"

"She is with me."

"Look in her eyes and see if it is someone you know in your present life."

"...Uh, no."

this can't be! it's samantha! i can't tell greg that i see samantha!

"Look at your children now. How many do you see?"

"Two."

"Are they people you know? Look in their eyes."

"Yes. One is Julia and the other one is her sister, Andrea."

"Why are you in the mountains?"

"We are hiding from soldiers. I can hear them coming...they are near.

hide children, hide!

"I hear my wife screaming! They are taking her away! I have to get to her...I am running behind the horses...the soldier is throwing Samantha off of his horse. I am leaning over her and I feel pain in my back...I am being hurt by something...I feel myself floating... fading."

"Where are you now?" Greg asked.

"Nowhere..."

"That's enough. I'm going to bring you back now. You will awaken and be completely rested. You will remember everything you saw and heard."

He began to count - 5, 4, slowly 3, 2, and 1.

I felt weak as I came out of the hypnosis, and I

lowered my head into my hands. I was totally confused. How could this be possible?

"Greg," I whispered, "I think my wife was Samantha...our Samantha in the next room, for God's sake."

"It's OK," Greg said. "It *is* real. You had a past life together and now you've come back to work through the karma. The children felt abandoned because they were left behind. You take good care of Julia now for a reason. You are here to make up for the past. And, now you know why you care so much about her sister."

Samantha came into the room and asked, "How did you do?"

Greg told her that we did fine, but I could say nothing. I was afraid to tell her what I knew.

Samantha hesitated for a second and sent an inquisitive smile my way.

"You know, the more I look at you, William, the more I have to admit - there's something very familiar about you."

I quickly answered, "Well, maybe you finally remember something from a few months ago at the fair."

Greg looked startled. Was he expecting more? I was *not* going to tell her anything.

We followed Samantha back to the living room to join the others for a short break before the group began to discuss their regressions. Several of the couples were eager to share, but I said nothing. In truth, I couldn't wait to get out of there. My appointment for a personal consultation with Samantha would have to wait until I could understand another unbelievable occurrence in my life.

CHAPTER SIX

My situation at home remained the same except for the fact that Julia began to question why I wasn't working. I simply could not explain to her, or to myself, why I wasn't returning to work. I went back to Dr. Jordan for a follow-up visit and my weight had dropped ten pounds. Other than that, I got a clean bill of health.

I told him that I was unable to return to work and I couldn't seem to pull myself together. He simply said I should give it a few more weeks and then return to the office several days a week, until I felt up to par.

Right.

and what's par, I wondered on the way back home. I decided that the weight fluctuation was because food wasn't important to me any more. I ate because the clock told me it was time for breakfast, lunch or dinner.

My mind drifted a lot. I thought about my reason for being on this earth. The images of my past-life regression sent me to search for facts on Indian tribes, their locations, their demise. I wrestled with the idea of making a call to Samantha for a consultation. In truth, I was afraid to be alone with her.

I decided to continue my classes with Rodney and hope that he and the group would be able to help me. My analytical mind was definitely not firing on all its cylinders, so I was hoping my psychic mind could provide some answers.

Instead of putting Julia in the healing circle, I put myself in the circle. Other members had done it in the past, and this time I knew it was my turn. I counted on the healing energy of my friends. The meditation that followed, however, turned out to be a waste of time. I got into the relaxation and fell asleep. It was embarrassing to admit when everyone else was telling his or her visions with such enthusiasm.

But then, an amazing thing happened. Rodney decided to play a color recognition game. He chose me to be his partner saying, "William, let's see if you can do this."

"You should try someone else, Rodney," I insisted. "I don't think I'm strong enough."

"Sure you are. Pull your chair over in front of mine."

I moved my chair as he asked and faced him. He handed me a folded piece of paper, saying he knew what color was marked on the inside. He asked me to tell him the color.

"William, the energy has to be perfect in this. Concentrate on the paper. Now get your energy in line with mine."

"I don't know what you mean," I insisted.

"You can do this, William. I know you can. Work with me. Close your eyes and let the energy flow through you."

I closed my eyes, and in a few minutes I said, "It's red."

I looked down and opened the paper. It was red!

"How did I do that? Can we do another one?"

We did another one, and another and another. I named each color correctly.

"Oh my God, Rodney. This is wonderful! I can

actually *do something*!"

"I had no doubt. I have information for you and I will share it with you when we have some private time. I'd like to take you with me to a seminar on Silva Mind Control this coming week. You're ready for it now. What do you think?"

I didn't even question his suggestion. Two days later, Rodney and I were in the front row of a three-day seminar on mind development and stress control. Some of the techniques paralleled what we were already doing with our meditation group. Our instructor, John Pettit, taught us relaxation techniques on day one, general self-improvement on day two, and sensory projection on the third day. Sensory projection is projecting the mind to find health problems within the body and sending healing energy to those areas. We were asked to bring 3 cards containing names, addresses, and ages of friends or relatives with specific health problems.

Rodney and I arrived for class on that final day with our sets of 3X5 cards, as did the other twenty students. Anticipation in the room was high, but our cards would have to wait until we received a full morning of preliminary instruction. Mr. Pettit took us down many times into the alpha state of relaxation until we could enter very quickly following his brief suggestion. We were told to envision a blank movie screen and put the people he named on that screen. A laboratory was to be invented in our minds to analyze and diagnose. We were also told to set up a *pretend* pharmacy with a magical pill that could cure any and all ills.

We were then instructed to scan the individuals and use healing energy in any form we knew would be effective, no matter how bizarre it seemed. Many names were presented to us in the training. To my amazement, I could see and scan them all. I had no doubt that Rodney got the same positive results.

We broke for a group luncheon and the conversation around the table was wild. This was an experience that we could use to benefit others for the rest of our lives. We returned excitedly to the classroom an hour later to test our newly discovered skills.

"Ladies and gentlemen," said Mr. Pettit, "our hard work is about to pay off. Please get comfortable now and relax. If you wish to leave your chair at this time and sit on the floor, you may do so. There are some pillows on the table at the back of the room."

One woman went to get a pillow and put it on the floor near our chairs.

"All right. We're ready to start. Close your eyes. To the count of three, put your thumb and your index finger together, and you will be at the level you need to achieve. One, two, three. You are putting up your screen. There is a woman on your screen at this time. She is 70 years old. Her name is Helene. Her location at this time is the 800 block of Burnett Avenue in Ames, Iowa, just 30 miles north of this room."

I thought my head would explode! I saw her immediately. I was totally amazed. How could I have this ability? When did it come to me? Information came tumbling in from my guides as I started at the crown chakra at the top of her head and scanned down her body. The guides were flagging a darkened area at her right shoulder.

i see a broken bone. there is a flag at the right elbow. i see bone splinters. i'm connecting the bones and filling them with green light. i'm scanning down now into the chest. i see a black area. i'm going deeper now into the left lung. my guide is telling me there is a tumor. i'm using a laser and burning out the tumor. i'm filling it with green light. i'm scanning down. my guides are flagging inflammation at the base of the spine - some at both knees. i'm burning out the inflammation with the laser and pushing marshmallows in between the vertebrae to cushions them. i'm looking over the body again. the healing is complete.

And then I heard Mr. Pettit say, "All right, you can come back now. You will feel rested and alert and you will remember everything you saw and did."

No one moved. No one spoke. I personally felt as if I had visited another time, another place, another Universe. After giving us time to acclimate, Mr. Pettit continued.

"Now I'll pass out paper and pencils. I want you to write down everything you found out about this 70 year-old female. When you've completed your observations, fold your papers and wait quietly until everyone has finished."

I was hyped. My pencil flew. I had to laugh when I wrote the part about the marshmallows, but I knew that my answers were right. I folded my paper and looked around. Some students were still writing.

rodney is going to die when he sees what I can do!

"Is everyone ready? I am going to tell you everything about our subject, and I want you to check off everything you got right."

I unfolded my paper and glanced at Rodney. He

was looking right back at me with a grin the size of Texas. "This 70 year-old female, named Helene, is my mother. She suffers from inflammatory arthritis of her lower back and knees. She's in pain all the time. She was trying to go to the basement to do the wash two weeks ago and fell down the stairs. She tried to break her fall, which is a natural reaction, and in the process, broke both her shoulder and elbow. She managed to get up the stairs and call for help. The CAT scan not only showed the broken bones, but it also showed a tumor about the size of a quarter in her left lung. A biopsy was taken and the tumor is malignant. However, as soon as she's feeling well enough, she'll begin chemotherapy. The doctors are optimistic about her recovery. So class, how did you do?"

Hands went up all over the room. Looks of astonishment were traded and my classmates were beaming. The percentage of hits was high. Rodney and I aced the test. We were thrilled! Mr. Pettit continued to question the class on its accuracy and went on to say it was time to share the names we brought to class.

"I want you to count off, one, two; one, two, so that you pair off with someone you don't know. Sit facing each other and get comfortable. Each of you will keep your own cards. You are to relax your partner when you begin by using the thumb and index finger technique.

"The two women directly in front of me - Ann and Lynn? Ann, you will begin by scanning the people listed on Lynn's three cards. She'll tell you whether or not you are correct. Then Lynn will scan your three cards, and you will tell her whether or not *she* is correct. When this is completed, look around the room to see which couple has finished, and switch partners. You will use your original cards with the new person, and he with you. We have the rest of the afternoon to work, so don't rush."

I remember one scanning in particular on that day. My partner presented a three year-old girl named Angela who also lived in the nearby city of Ames. I reported the following:

"My guide is showing me Angela. She has thinning reddish-blonde hair. She's in a lot of pain, and she does not smile. My guide is flagging pain throughout her body. I'm wrapping her entire body in green light from the top of her head, down over her shoulders, down her arms and across her chest, down over her abdomen, down her legs and around her feet.

"My guide is showing me black spots throughout her body. I'm shooting laser beams of purple healing light to every black spot that is flagged."

When it was over, I told my partner that the child had leukemia and had been undergoing chemotherapy for some time. I saw cancer in her grandfather who had passed on, but whose spirit was standing just behind her right shoulder. I don't know how I was able to detect her grandfather, but he was there. My partner told me I was correct; she told me that she was the mother of the child.

We left the Silva training school on that Thursday, deeply affected by our experiences - deeply affected by what we developed in those three days that would benefit others. As we drove, I told Rodney about Angela.

"I asked Mrs. Roth for her phone number, Rodney. I want to continue the healing from my home, and I want to call and check on Angela's progress. Do you think it was OK to get the number?"

"Absolutely. You're very strong, and I think you

should start working on Angela immediately. Everyone we work with in the future will benefit from this knowledge."

Rodney and I developed a close friendship after spending those three days together. He told me he became a "seer" immediately after he left Samantha's healing couch. So, not only was he gifted with perfect speech, but he was also given insight to help others.

His job by day was that of a computer programmer, and he was fortunate to be able to work out of his home. This gave him the time he needed to work with individuals who came to get help. I suggested perhaps he could try the "physician, heal thyself" method and cure his terrible smoking habit before it killed him, but he laughed and said he had smoked since his teen years and enjoyed smoking too much to quit.

The following Sunday at our group meditation, we shared the knowledge with our friends, and Rodney outlined several scannings that he had done with his partners. I told of only one - Angela.

They listened with interest as I outlined Angela's case plus the fact that I continued to work on her from home. I told them I called Angela's mother before I came to class and she told me the pain was less severe - at least there were fewer complaints.

"This is strange, though," I added, "Mrs. Roth told me that her daughter has not been herself. She's not the little girl she was before her illness. She has a filthy mouth, of all things, and she is only three years old. There's no way she could know those words.

"The doctor tells her that Angela is very angry and upset because she's in continual pain. He says depression almost always results from chemo and that depression at any age can cause all sorts of abnormal behavior."

And then I dropped the bomb - I had seen something else as I scanned Angela's tiny body.

"I wonder if any of you will have an answer for me," I proposed. "I saw actual *figures* attached to her and they had no faces. I just wondered, well, could they be some kind of angels? Angels trying to help her?"

No one in the room spoke up. Not even Rodney. I looked at my friends and waited for an answer - any answer. Finally, there was a suggestion.

"You should call Samantha about that."

Monday morning I sat at the kitchen table with my cup of coffee. I barely noticed Julia moving around. My mind was racing. No way could I call Samantha. I would be worried every minute that she'd see something in my face that would give me away. Something that would give her a clue, spark her memory of a time we might have spent together. Yet, I knew very well that this kind of self-ishness would not help Angela Roth.

CHAPTER SEVEN

Around 11:30, I put on my nicer shorts and shirt, grabbed the newspaper, and headed for my favorite taco restaurant for lunch. For some reason, I decided to try something different and stopped at a cafeteria right off the Interstate. I got in line and decided on mashed potatoes, chicken fried steak and a salad. There was a booth open along the front window, and it was mine.

I was just opening my newspaper when I heard someone say, "Are you alone?"

geez, louise!

"Samantha! Yes, I'm here alone. Please, sit down!" I scrambled to get out of the booth and I took her tray.

"Thanks, " she said, and she slid in on the other side. She was wearing a pale green sweater that highlighted her eyes and black jeans that fit exactly right.

"This is a coincidence, Samantha. I never came in here before. Do you come here often?"

"I come here quite often, as a matter of fact. I like the food here, and I live just down the street."

"Me too! Well, sort of. I live less than a mile from here...another coincidence, I guess."

I picked up my fork and my hand was visibly shaking. I looked up at her, but she had begun to eat, so I felt that she hadn't noticed my nervousness. Then a strange thing happened. She opened a casual conversation, and within a few minutes, we were talking as if we had known each other forever. We were finishing each other's sentences. I was telling her things about myself that I never thought I could tell anyone.

It was only a matter of time before I began to tell her the story of my experiences at the Silva training course and about Angela, my special child.

She listened intently and said, "I just finished a course myself - on depossession. It can help your Angela."

"*Depossession*? That's the work of the Devil. What are you saying?"

"No, William. You have it all wrong. The *figures* you're seeing attached to Angela's body are entities. They don't belong there. They're taking her energy and she can't get well. You and I can work together and remove them by doing a depossession. We don't have to have Angela in the room with us to do it. Would you agree to that?"

"I can use my Silva, can't I. Yes, I'd love to try to help her. How soon can we begin?"

"Can you come to my house tomorrow morning?"

"That would be wonderful. Is ten too early?"

"Ten will be fine. I'll give you my card."

She scribbled an address on the back of her business card and passed it to me. I smiled and thanked her, and she excused herself to leave.

"I'm just happy that I can help, William. I have a feeling we'll be able to work well together."

At ten the next morning I pulled into her driveway and parked next to her brown Dodge Caravan. She lived in a Spanish style, white stucco home near the middle of the block. When she opened the door, I was met with the fragrance of sage. When I commented, she said she liked to burn sage or incense in the evening while working or relaxing with a good book. She had a fireplace, cozy burgundy corduroy couches, bookcases on two walls, and large groupings of Indian artifacts. Candles in a multitude of sizes and colors were on the dark wooden tables and fresh flowers from her garden were strewn in a basket on the hearth.

Samantha was dressed in casual khaki slacks and a purple silk shirt, but bare-footed, which took me a little by surprise. I followed her into a back bedroom, which had been converted into her workroom. It was carpeted with woven cotton rag rugs and furnished with two black leather armchairs and an indirect lamp. There was a gray computer station along one wall and a cork bulletin board running the entire distance above the work area. It was overgrown with notes, photos and sheets of correspondence.

Samantha asked me to have a seat and she opened a drawer to produce a yellow legal pad. She drew a stick figure to represent Angela's body in the center of the cover sheet and wrote the child's name and address at the top of the page.

I felt comfortable in her house, but I felt inferior to her presence.

"I know I can do this work with you, but you'll have to give me some instructions," I reminded her.

"I have confidence in your ability, William. Your accuracy from the Silva classes you told me about yesterday is a good indication that you have a gift. We may end up with an excellent working relationship. Are you ready to give it a try?"

"Yes, I'm ready," I said, as I settled back into one of the chairs and relaxed my hands on my lap.

Samantha began with, "I'll turn on the tape recorder so that we can review our work when we finish. After you are down, I will ask you to scan Angela and tell me exactly what your guides are showing you. As you pinpoint the darkened areas, you will tell me their exact locations and I'll mark them on this yellow sheet. Then we will go back to the top of the drawing and work through all of the areas with the help of your guide.

"We are bringing in God's white light to protect us. It will circle us and fill up the room completely. You will touch your thumb to your index finger on the count of three. One...two...three. I want you to send a portion of yourself out. You are finding Angela Roth. You will find her at home with her mother on Ontario Avenue in Ames, Iowa. Do you see Angela?"

"I see Angela," I replied.

"I want you to ask Angela's higher self if we have permission to do this."

"Yes, we do."

"OK. Now, I ask you to scan Angela's body from top to bottom, looking for any energies or any negative souls that may be there. Tell me what you see, feel, and what they say. In the name of Jesus Christ, they cannot hide, and they must come forward. Your scan will be able to detect them."

"There's a man standing in her space," I said. "The aura is gray around the top of her head. There's a dark spot in her solar plexus and another dark area on her right ankle."

"Let's go up to the top of Angela's head now, William. Concentrate your attention there. I'm speaking to any entities that are causing this gray mass around

50

Angela's head. In the name of Jesus, you must come forward and speak to William, or speak through him, and give him your thoughts. Let him speak for you. I will count, one, two, three. Who are you? Do you have a name?"

"I don't need to speak to you."

"All right then," said Samantha, "we ask that the forces of Michael the Archangel throw a net around this one - a net of light - and confine this and any others like him in Angela until we can speak to him. Hold the net tightly until he speaks to me with a little respect.

"You need to speak to me now because you are trapped like a fish in a net. We can pull the net tighter and make it hurt, so you better speak to me. What are you doing around Angela's head?"

"It's a place to stay."

"Ok, it's a place to stay. Well, you can't stay there any more. Today is moving day. This is Angela's space, not yours, and there's a law in the Universe that says this space belongs to her and not to you. So, you must leave."

"She wasn't using that space."

"She wasn't using that space? I am telling you that the space is still hers. It does not belong to you. Do you have a name?"

"I don't need to tell you my name."

"Well, I suggest you might want to because you are here in this net and you can't get loose until we allow you to be released. You must speak to me with respect. If you have a name, do you know if you ever had an earth body?"

"Yah, I have one now."

"No you *don't*! This is Angela's body - a little 3

year-old girl's body - and you're hurting her by being in there. What was your job? What was your assignment? What were you told to do in Angela's head?"

"I can stay here until I move on."

"Do you have any special reason for hurting her in any way? Were you told to do anything to her?"

"I'm not telling you that."

"You must speak to me respectfully. OK, please pull the net a little tighter until this one begins to feel the pressure. We can tighten the net until you are under great stress...pain. You've been discovered. Who sent you? Please pull the net tighter; make this one squirm a little bit."

"I don't like this."

"I know you don't like this. It can get worse, believe me. Now if you speak to me, we will loosen the net a little bit, but you must be truthful. Do you understand? You've been discovered. Who sent you?"

"You know where I come from. I will not say."

"I think I know where you come from. What I'm going to do is remind you that you've been discovered. What happens to those of you who are discovered?"

"It's a dark place."

"A dark place? Is it pain? Suffering? Have you ever been to the place of punishment?"

"No."

"You've heard about it though..."

"Yes."

"Well, I could let you go but I think your boss, the one who sent you, would take you to that place right away because you've been discovered. I think you were told that you were not to be discovered. Were you promised anything if you stayed here for a while?"

"Yes."

"OK. You don't have to go with him because I'm going to suggest another option. Are you willing to listen to that option?"

"Yes."

"All right. Look at these beings who have you in this nct. What do they look like?"

"Like light."

"Would you like to be with them - where there's no punishment? They live in a place where there's no punishment or pain. They don't spend their time hurting little children like Angela. They spend their time helping people. Does that seem like a better deal? Never being punished? Always giving help?"

"They just tell you that."

"No, I'm telling you the truth. You've been told so many lies that you don't even believe the truth when you hear it. You had better pay close attention because we don't have a lot of time to waste on you. You're going to have to make a decision very soon. You can go away to the light. Perhaps you can be retrained and find something good about yourself."

"What is the light?"

"What have you been told about the light?"

"Burns."

"I'm going to prove that's a lie. Somebody's been telling you some lies, here. All right now...I'm going to ask that a shaft of light be sent through this being. And another, and another, and another and another. Now, did that burn you?"

"No."

"It didn't burn you. It didn't do any harm at all, did it? It was just another lie."

"Why doesn't it burn?"

"It doesn't burn because the light is good. The light will not harm you. You've been lied to and told to avoid the light. There are some things about the light that are so good and your dark master doesn't want you to know about them. He doesn't want you to know because you will want to go to the light."

"I can't find it."

"The light? Yes, you can find it."

"He will find me."

"Do you know he can't find you here in this net? He can't harm you in any way."

"Do I have to stay here - here in this net?"

"No. You can be free from the net once you've changed yourself - once you've allowed yourself to be light like these other beings. Then the dark one can't reach you any more, and you will be free to travel in the light. The dark one only hurts people who are confused, or naïve or hurting. So, when you have your act together, he can't hurt you at all. Do you have a friend in there with you?"

"Yes."

"Has he heard what we've been saying? Is he interested in going to the light with you and discovering some new adventures?"

"Yes."

"All right. You have to look deep inside yourself and ask your friend to look deep inside of himself. There is a light that has always been with you but it is something you never realized. It has always been there."

"I see a light."

"What does the light look like?"

"It's like a little fire."

"Ok, let the fire begin to grow. As you concentrate on the fire, it will grow. Is it growing? Keep concentrating. Somehow, some way, dark deeds and dark thoughts have almost extinguished the fire. Are you willing to let that flame grow until you are shining also?"

"Yes, I am."

"Tell me when it is completed. Tell me when you are totally consumed by that wonderful light."

"Yes."

"What about your friend?"

"Yes."

"Now, you can leave. We are going to let these light beings take you with them, but we want you to go willingly. We want you to go to a place in the light where you can be trained and taught the ways of the light beings. You will hear the truth. You will never fear punishment. You will be in a new place. Maybe you can come back and help another who was like you.

"You are free to go, and as you leave, call to the Universe for any dark ones who want to come along. Now I want you to look closely at Angela. Look in her aura and look in her body. Are there any others who want to come? They've all been told that they can go free. Are there any who want to go with you? Maybe they are tired of being lied to. There are any more?"

"Do they have to be in this body?"

"No. They can be nearby; they can be anywhere in the Universe. As you leave now, call out to them. Ask them to look deep inside themselves for that little speck of light. It will begin to grow, and they can follow you to the light where they will be safe. Are any coming with you?"

"Yes."

"How many?"

"Many."

"Take many with you - those of same stature, lesser stature or greater stature - anyone who wants to come. But each must find that light within himself before he is allowed to go. I thank you for leaving and helping Angela. It's a good way for you to start your new life. Go with God; go in peace.

"Now we call on the Angels of Light to fill in those vacated spaces within Angela - filling Angela's body and the aura around her head. Fill those spaces with light until they are bubbling over into the rest of her body. Fill until they consume her entire body and totally protect her in one continual light."

"Now, William, we are going to focus on the solar plexus. I'm calling for any energy or person who is in the solar plexus of Angela - on the count of three, come forward. One, two, three. Who are you? In the name of Jesus, I command you. You must speak to me. One, two, three. Speak to me. What is your name?"

"Cindy."

"All right, Cindy. Did you ever have an earth body?"

"Yes."

"When did you join Angela? How long ago?"

"When she was two."

"Cindy, why did you join her? Were you trying to help her, or hurt her in some way?"

"No, I didn't want to hurt her."

"How old were you at that time?"

"When I lost my body?"

"Yes."

"When I was about four years old."

"And, did you wander around for a while before you found Angela?"

"Yes."

"What were your feelings? Were you afraid?"

"I was scared, and there was nobody...so I lived with Angela."

"Did Angela know you were there?"

"Sometimes we talk."

"You're like one of her playmates, or something?"

"We talk sometimes."

"Well, Honey, you can't stay here any longer, OK? I know you don't mean to hurt her, but just by being there, you are draining her energy. You're hurting her in some way. So, this is what we are going to do...we will ask someone you remember when you were living, or a spirit who knows you and cares about you, to come and help you. Does that sound OK?"

"Somebody will be there? I won't be by myself?"

"I'll ask someone from the light who knows you or cares about you to come right now. Please be in front of Cindy and take her hand. Look in her eyes and show yourself so she is not afraid. We don't want her wandering around."

"See Mimi."

"Your mother?"

"My gramma."

"Oh, your gramma! How does that make you feel, Cindy?"

"That's nice. I want to go with my gramma."

"OK, all right...Gramma's going to take you to a really neat place and later you can have a body of your own and you won't be hurting Angela. You will be really happy with your gramma. Now, tell Angela goodbye.

"OK, Cindy, we will say goodbye to her for you, and I'm sure she loves you too. Are there others there around you that you can see who want to come with you? Ask them if they want to come. Look around. Inside and outside of Angela's body."

"There's just one by her ankle, but he's a *crab*!"

"OK."

"I don't think he will want to come with me."

"Well, we will take care of him later. Now, you just go on with your gramma. Go in peace; go in love, and I'm sure you will be happy. OK?"

"OK."

"Thanks for leaving and helping Angela. Go with God; go in peace. Tell me when she's gone, William."

"Now."

"All right. Now focus your attention on the dark spot in her aura on her right ankle. Cindy said he's a real crab. In the name of Jesus, I command you. Speak to me now. What is your name?"

"Jerod."

"How long have you been with Angela?"

"For about - not too long - maybe a couple years."

"Why are you crabby?"

"Cause I don't like kids."

"Why did you come in with a child? Were you aware of what you were doing?"

"Well, no wonder I'm crabby! She's a kid!"

"Jerod, can you think back to the time when you might have had a body?"

"Yes."

"And, in what State were you living? What area of the World?"

"What area of the World?"

"Well, yes. Where did you live?"

"I lived in Iowa."

"How old were you?"

"Seventy."

"And, did you go into the hospital, or have an accident or something?"

"I was in the old-folks home."

"Do you remember losing your body?"

"Yes."

"How did that make you feel?"

"Real bad. I didn't want to just float around."

"You didn't know what to do? Well, I guess you joined Angela sometime after that."

"She came visiting her grandpa at the old-folks home and I hung on. I thought maybe she'd take me somewhere good, but the kid never does."

"Jerod, if you want to go somewhere good, you're talking to the right lady because I can get you transferred out of here. How does that sound?"

"That sounds good. Do I get somebody other than a kid?"

"Oh, you can have your *own* body. And, not an old one, either. You can get one that is about twenty-five, or something. We're going to get you a good one."

"One that's not all used up?"

"We are going to get you one that's young and spry

59

so you can get out and run and jump and play again."

"Chase them women!"

"You can do that again, too. I'll tell you what...if you want to leave, I will ask someone from the light to come for you. I am calling for someone Jerod remembers - someone Jerod trusts. Show yourself and look in his eyes. Jerod, who are you seeing?"

"My brother, Phil."

"How does that make you feel?"

"Real happy to see him."

"OK. Does he look good?"

"Looks good."

"Jerod I want you to talk to Phil for just a second and he'll tell you about the light...the place he's going to take you. Do you think you want to go there?"

"Yep."

"It sounds better than this, doesn't it?"

"Oh, yes."

"Do you want to say anything to Angela? You were kind of holding her back a little bit, you know."

"Sorry, kid."

"We ask you to go with God, go with light, go with love, and go in peace. Tell me when he's gone, William."

"He's gone."

"All right now, what I'm going to do is use a giant fine-mesh net. Nothing and no one can hide within it. I want to run it over Angela's aura, down over her head and over her whole body. A huge ball of light will be trapped within it. I am running it all the way down to the knees, ankles, feet and toes.

"And now, we ask the Angels of Light to pour light on Angela. She is a child of God; she is a child of the light. She has great things to do in this lifetime and we ask this light to be overflowing and bubbling and nothing can take its place. We are filling the vacated spaces with light and love so nothing can return. We are filling the aura at arms length - two feet above her and two feet below her."

"Tell me when she is totally full of light, William."

"She is totally full of light."

"Great. We ask you, William, to give Angela's higher self permission to realize she will feel different until she gets used to this change."

"She will."

"William, I ask you to return here and scan your own body. Now I will put this very fine golden mesh over your aura and over your body to cleanse you - to make sure nothing is hanging on. I am bringing it over your head, your shoulders, your chest, your hips, your knees, your feet, your ankles and your toes. Is there anything trapped in that net?"

"No."

"Good. We ask that the light be totally dispersed in your body and mind, overflowing so nothing negative can come to you. William, I ask you now to do the same for me."

"It is done."

"William, the next time we work together, I will say the words, *Blue Rose*, and you will immediately be at the level you have to reach to begin our work. I'm going to bring you out of it. I will count from five. Five, you are becoming aware of your breathing; four, you are coming up further to the sounds in the room; three, the sound of my voice; two...one...open your eyes when you are ready."

I sat quietly. I felt mellow but somewhat confused. It took a moment to get myself together before I opened my eyes.

Samantha was radiant. "You did very well, William. I had no idea. How do you feel?"

"I feel all right, but I don't remember anything I said. I just hope we helped Angela."

"I can assure you we did," she replied. "Can you stay for a while and review the tape recording?"

"I'm dying to find out what's on that tape. Can I take you to lunch after we finish? You've been so generous to do this for me."

"Absolutely. You'll be pleased with what you were able to do."

Was I ever! It was the most amazing thing I ever heard. My voice actually sounded childlike when I was speaking for Cindy, who was attached to Angela's solar plexus, and Jerod's voice was certainly not my own. I was delighted that I was capable of such work. We talked excitedly about each action and reaction in the depossession as it rolled from the tape. When it was over, I wanted to hear more.

We left her house for lunch and we both knew in our hearts that we had done an excellent job. We chose the same window seat at the same cafeteria near the Interstate, and our lunch stretched into three hours. Neither of us realized how much time had passed. As we talked, she became more serious with me about her work and wanted me to know that our connection was not an accident.

"We have done this work before in another lifetime. We worked smoothly as one entity."

I didn't understand what she was saying. Could she have been referring to the Indian/soldier scenario I experienced in my regression with Gregory? I made no reply and she continued:

"I get cases like this all the time, William, and I need someone to scan my clients. Will you work with me?"

"Oh, I'd love to, Samantha. I feel totally invigorated, and I'd love to work with you again. You can call me any time."

"That's wonderful, William...how about tomorrow?"

"Tomorrow?"

"I have four cases. We may not get to all of them in one day so I may need you for several days. I'll even throw in lunch if you help me - lunch right here by the window."

"It's a deal. What time should I show up?"

"How about nine in the morning? And, if you're doing half the work, I'll split the fee with you."

"How much do you charge?" I asked. It surprised me that she offered to share her income.

"I charge sixty dollars. People always try to pay me more because the results have been phenomenal. You'll see for yourself when you call Mrs. Roth this afternoon. I've helped children who were on the verge of being committed because they appeared to be mentally ill. When you scan for me tomorrow, it won't be necessary to tell you what symptoms brought the client to us. All you will need is the name and the location.

"When our work has been completed, the client will realize he has experienced wonderful changes. In some cases, however, he will invite the entities back because he prefers the twisted rewards of his previous behavior. He is dealing with lessons he came here to learn, and his pain and illness are a part of that. You will always ask for permission to work, and if you don't get it, we will back off immediately."

"If you have four people waiting for help, how did you get their names?"

"I work with those who have tried every avenue. Somehow they find me. I guess you could say word-of-mouth, mostly, because I have been very successful. And you and I will be able to accomplish even more as a team. I can't tell you how happy I am that you told me about Angela."

"This is a wonderful opportunity for me, Samantha. I'm the one who should be grateful. You opened a window for me in more ways than one because I didn't know what was happening in my life. I can see a direction now.

"You couldn't possibly remember this, but when you did my reading at the Embassy Suites, you said I was on a path to help others. At the time, I knew I was helping others through therapy as a psychologist, but I had no idea what was in store for me. I have a few life-decisions to make."

We parted in her driveway and I drove home to call Mrs. Roth. My hands were shaking as I picked up the phone.

"Mrs. Roth?"

"Yes."

"This is William from the Silva class. I just called to ask about Angela. How is she doing today?"

my god, i'm trembling.

"Oh, William, how nice of you to call. Angela is napping right now. She had a nice lunch with me and said she was sleepy and walked down the hall and crawled into bed."

"How is her appetite?"

"She ate pretty well, actually. I was a little surprised. Her appetite hasn't been very good."

"How about the pain?"

"She didn't say much about that. She was tired and wanted to take a nap."

"Oh, OK. Well, I ran into a friend of mine who helped me do a depossession on Angela and I am hoping that you will see some differences."

"You did *what*?"

"Let me explain. Sometimes spirits attach to a person and they don't mean any harm. Angela did have some spirits attached, and we removed them with a deposession. It was perfectly safe, Mrs. Roth. You should be noticing a positive change in her behavior."

"I'll watch her tonight, and I'll let you know."

The evening wore on and there was no call. I fought back the urge to call Mrs. Roth again. I thought the worst.

But the call came. It came at 8:00 the next morning.

"William, guess what! Angela didn't complain to me about pain at all last night. I'm so excited! And she slept very well...didn't wake up crying for the first time in ...I don't know how long. I just had to call you. She's eating her breakfast now, and she seems very happy. Isn't it good news? I have to go now, but I'll call you later. Thanks so much, William."

A month later, Mrs. Roth did call again. Angela's tests were showing a remission. Her outlook was better.

CHAPTER EIGHT

I continued to do depossessions with Samantha on a regular basis and Samantha came to Rodney's occasionally for our meditations. She eventually stopped attending because she felt the members were not developing their own potential. They were looking to her for all of their answers.

One Sunday evening, just before the group was scheduled to arrive, Rodney and I decided to give them a challenge. We would have them concentrate on the neighbor's house across the street. Peculiar things had been happening there for years, and we thought it would be interesting to bring up the problem in class. When everyone was settled into a relaxation and we had protected ourselves in the white light, Rodney set the stage.

"Tonight we will focus on the house directly across the street from where we are sitting. Many different families have lived in the home. They all came in as happy families, and one by one, they left because of divorce or trouble with their children. Police show up at all hours of the day and night to follow up on complaints from neighbors or from the residents themselves.

"Now, this is the part that intrigues me: the owner came over to see me a few days ago, saying, 'I saw the silhouette of a girl walking down the hall and it vanished into thin air. It was like a vapor. What do you think? Could it be a ghost? Is there anything you can do to help me get rid of it?'

"So, with that in mind, I want you to travel across

the street to #112. You are looking at the house. You are now entering by the front door. You are walking into the main room of the house. You are moving about the interior, looking in every room, opening every closet while traveling from the front to the rear of the house. If any one of you sees a lost soul, ask it to speak to you. Find out why it is there and what it wants."

It was very quiet in the room. I saw the house and entered as directed. I saw the soul immediately. She was a young girl, Caucasian, wearing an ankle-length cotton dress and no shoes. She had long, straight brown hair.

"I see her," I said.

"Yes, William," answered Rodney, "where is she?"

"I am in the first room and I see her in a hallway. The hall leads to a back room - possibly a bedroom."

"Call to her," said Rodney.

I called to her, and at that point, Rodney took over asking questions. I began to speak for the child as her spirit communicated to me.

"What is your name?" Rodney asked.

"Mattie Jo," I said.

"How old are you?"

"Eight."

"Where are you?"

"I'm hiding."

"Why are you hiding?"

"I'm hiding from the Indians."

"Do you see a bright light?" Rodney asked.

"No."

"Look around you."

"I see it."

"Walk toward the light. You will be safe in there.

The Indians will not get you."

"No, I want to stay here."

"Why do you want to stay there, Mattie Jo?"

"I want to stay with my *body*."

"Mattie Jo, you are free to walk to the light. You can have a new body. You will be happy in the light. I now call for someone who knows Mattie Jo to come from the light. Look around, Mattie Jo. Do you recognize anyone? Do you see your mother or your father?"

"No. I want to stay here...stay here with my body."

"Now, Mattie Jo, I will tell you one more time. Look toward the light. Walk to the light. You will be safe in the light."

"No. I am happy here with my body. Oh, there's my *mommy*!"

"All right, Mattie Jo. Before you go, do you see any others around you that want to go with you now?"

"No."

"All right, you may go to your mommy. Go in peace; go with God.

"William, let me know when she's gone."

"She is gone."

"Good. Now, William, you may move out of the main room and back out of the front door. Cross the street and return to us at this time. For you and all the others in the room, I'm counting back from three - three...two...one...please open your eyes when you are ready."

Smiles erupted around the room as Rodney continued with, "We can see literally hundreds in line when we call out for anyone else who wishes to cross over. It surprises me that none were around Mattie Jo. We must con-

69

tinue to do everything in our power to help those who wish our help."

Rodney's wife, Barbara, added, "You know, there were Indians all over this area with Fort Atkinson, Fort Dodge and Fort Madison. I think it would be excellent to call in as many Indian spirits as we can at one of our meetings. Why don't we build a bonfire down by the lake and we will have our own pow-wow? Let's do it as soon as the weather warms up a little more."

Days with Samantha and Sunday evenings with the group became the highlights of my life as Julia's condition remained unchanged. Our relationship became more distant. Each evening was the same even though I did not work evenings as I had in the past. She came in after school, ate or drank her dinner and passed out. I begged her to return to AA meetings or go to counseling, but she laughed at me and told me if I didn't like it, I could get out. More and more I found myself thinking about getting out. I was sick of it.

One evening I went to bed early. I had not had a particularly tiring day, but for some reason, I was exhausted. I woke up at 1:00 in the morning shaking, almost convulsing. I thought I was getting another bout of the flu. I got up to go to the bathroom and there was blood on the sheets that had been under me. I panicked! I guess I should have called Dr. Jordan, but I automatically called Samantha. She answered on the first ring.

"Samantha? Thank goodness you're awake. You have to help me."

"William, what's wrong?"

"I don't know what's happening. I'm bleeding. I woke up, and I smelled a chicken house; I smelled alcohol. I don't know what's happening to me."

"I'll be right over. What's your address?"

She was at my door in ten minutes. I didn't realize how much I needed her reassuring hug. We went to the living room. I sat in the recliner and she moved a smaller chair up next to me.

"We have to get you calmed down before we can do anything. I'm going to relax you now."

And she said, "*Blue Rose.*"

I could feel my body calming and the shaking stopped. I drifted down into blackness as Samantha spoke.

"Now we are going to go back into time and back to the chicken house."

"I don't want to go there! Please don't make me go there!"

"I am right here with you. It will be OK."

"I can see the chicken house."

"OK, let's go in. Remember I am with you. How old are you, William?"

"Four."

"Do you know where you are?"

"Yes."

"Tell me where you are."

"I am at Aunt Ellen's house."

"Well, what are you doing in the chicken house?"

"Gathering eggs because I am a good boy."

"Let's leave the chicken house now and go into Aunt Ellen's house. How did you get to Aunt Ellen's house?"

"I rode on the bus. I can ride the bus all by myself."

"You rode the bus *by yourself*?"

"Yes, and I walked up the hill and they have a swing. And I sat on the swing with my elephant."

"What kind of elephant did you sit with?"

"My stuffed elephant. And I can see Uncle Bernie coming up the hill. He's coming home from work and I get to go out and help him get the eggs from the chicken house."

"Then what happens? Where are you?"

"I'm in the chicken house. I'm in the chicken house with Uncle Bernie and he says I'm a good boy. I get to shoo the chickens off their nests and get the eggs. And his bottle is under one of the nests. And he is drinking from his bottle. He says good little boys do things for their uncles so they can come to the chicken house. He asked if I was a good little boy. I like to be a good little boy. I like to play with the chickens."

"William, remember I am with you. I am right here. What is Uncle Bernie doing to you?"

"He's hurting me!"

"Why do you think he's hurting you?"

"I don't know. I am being a good boy. I am doing what he tells me to do but it is hurting me and I am crying. I am screaming at my Aunt Ellen and she doesn't hear me. I am in the kitchen with her and I am screaming and she doesn't hear me!"

"It's OK, William. She can't hear you because you left your body and she can't hear you screaming. She can't help you because she can't hear you."

"Let's go back to your body. What is happening now?"

"He's cleaning me up, but it still hurts. But I am a

very good boy, and I will not tell anybody or I will not be able to come back to the chicken house and play with the chickens and collect the eggs. If I tell, everyone will think I am a bad boy and did not do what I was supposed to do."

"Ok, William, I'm going to bring you back now."

I had tears streaming down my face as I got out of the recliner and went over to the couch. Samantha came over and sat down next to me. She put her arm around my shoulder and I lowered my head in shame. I looked up at her and saw tears in her eyes, and I knew she felt my pain.

"This may have been more difficult for you than it was for me," I said softly.

"William, I know I'm supposed to remain objective, but it isn't easy. We have to discuss this. You were not reviewing a past life. It was your present life."

"Well, I always knew I had some missing time, Samantha. I truly can't remember some years."

"How many years do you think you lost?"

"I guess my whole childhood until I was about nine years old."

"How do you know?"

"Well, it started when someone asked me about Christmas at my house when I was little, and I couldn't remember Christmas. I have trouble remembering *anything* about those years."

"Tell me how you're feeling now, William."

"I've calmed down a lot. I feel much better."

"Do you think you're still bleeding?"

"I guess I should check."

I left the room. I didn't feel any embarrassment with Samantha - there just wasn't any. The tears were starting again and I was not sure if it was because

Samantha would be leaving, or if I was feeling the emotions of my experience.

"Thank you so much for coming over and helping me, Samantha," I said, as I returned to the living room. The bleeding has stopped."

"We should both get some sleep, William. We can work on this tomorrow. If you need me any more tonight, please call and I'll come back."

I thanked her, and as we reached the door, I put my arms around her. We held on to each other briefly, but I felt as if I were clinging for dear life.

I slept late the next day and called Samantha around 11:00 a.m. to ask if I could take her to lunch to repay her kindness from the night before. I picked her up at noon and we headed for the cafeteria. My food could wait, but my gratitude was spilling over.

"Samantha, you opened up my past last night - memories I'd suppressed. You have to know how thankful I am."

"Before you say any more, William, there is something I want to tell you. I could feel your pain last night and I'm sure we are soul mates."

"What?"

"I suspected that we were soul mates, but it may go even deeper."

"Deeper is right, Samantha."

It was finally time to tell her about the episode at Rodney's when my past-life regression showed her as my wife. She was not surprised. In fact, the story verified what she already knew and had planned to share with me. It was mind boggling, to say the least. It was more than I was prepared to deal with at this time in my life.

74

Samantha and I continued to work together, and we became closer in our personal relationship. We were almost like one person. We returned to the chicken house many times until I could accept the fact that it was true and could let it go. I was able to understand that my uncle was from the hills of Tennessee and believed that there was nothing wrong with his conduct. I was eventually able to forgive him in my heart and travel back to the family home to place flowers on his grave.

CHAPTER NINE

Rodney and Barbara's Indian pow-wow was postponed week after week due to rainy weather until Rodney finally picked the perfect night. The sky was filled with stars and the moon was nearly full. It was an unforgettable experience. I asked Samantha to go along with me, and we arrived to find a campfire blazing at the base of Rodney's property. Crazy Rodney and his snacks - it was an old-fashioned wiener roast with hot dogs, chips, and marshmallows.

He had dug a fire pit out of the earth and surrounded it with large, flat stones, similar to the campfires of the Indians. After we ate, we spread our blankets in a circle around the fire. We brought in the light of protection and invited any Indian spirits to join us.

Rodney led the group, and we all slipped quietly into meditation. His daughter, Suzanne, was there to drum softly in the background. Suddenly, I could see them coming out of the woods - *Indians*! They encircled the fire. In the meditation, the Indians appeared to be dancing, and Larry and Scott came out of meditation and did the simplest Indian dance they could imagine. Rodney called it, *The Gopher Stomp*.

I don't remember awakening at all, but when it was over, I found myself 20 yards away at the bank of Rodney's pond. I'll never understand how that happened. We talked at length later around the smoldering firewood about the messages some of us received. We described the Indians and realized several of us were describing the same people, so we had no idea of the total number that visited our campfire that night.

We all laughed when Rodney sneaked over to get a fourth hot dog. His pony, Beauty, had been wandering the property while we were in our meditation and had eaten all the rest of the hot dogs and marshmallows. Rodney and Barbara were not laughing. They told us Beauty would be sick if we didn't do something about her digestion, so we nabbed the guilty party with hot-dog breath. Who would have thought a licensed psychologist would end his career sending healing energy to a horse? Amid the laughter, Samantha invited all of us to visit her at the next psychic fair in Ames. It was scheduled for the following weekend.

When I arrived at the fair with lunch in hand, Samantha was waiting to meet me in the hotel lobby. We sat together in a vacant conference room and ate chicken salad sandwiches, potato chips and drank cokes, as we chattered about anything and everything. I enjoyed every moment with Samantha - such a beautiful, talented woman.

"William, we have open lecture hours that haven't been filled. Will you give a lecture for us? It will take about 1/2 hour of your time."

"What do you want me to talk about?"

"Surprise me. Just open your mouth and let it flow."

"OK. Are you going to come in and listen to me?"

"Sure."

She checked the lecture schedule and within an hour my name was called and guests were filling the lecture room. I stood at the podium, looked at the group seated in front of me and said, "I'd like to tell you about past-life regression." And I was off and running. She was right. The words came out of nowhere.

Samantha had taken a chair at the rear of the room and, before long, I saw her waving her arm. She wanted me to stop talking because my time was up and it was her turn. I smiled at her and brought my lecture to a close.

As I passed her in the aisle, I whispered, "What are you going to lecture on?"

"Soul mates!" she laughed.

She began with, "Thank you very much, William. Your lecture was excellent."

And then, "William is new to the fairs, and for those of you who have not met him personally, you will find him quite interesting in another respect. He is my soul mate... and probably more. And so I would like to speak to you today about soul mates and perhaps you will be able to get an insight on when, how, and whether or not you will be able to identify your own soul mate."

I sat mesmerized as Samantha smiled my way and continued her lecture.

"A soul mate is someone you meet and you know immediately that you have met that person before. Something triggers a memory inside of you. It may be a look, a face, a body structure or a word. You were with this person in many lifetimes as a brother/sister, mother/daughter, husband/wife, father/son or friend/friend.

"There is an unbelievable connection; there are remarkably strong feelings. Your soul mate understands you, disregards your faults and is there for you without judgement in times of joy and disappointment.

"How can you find your soul mate? I don't think

you can expect to just look around and *find* such a person. The soul mate will appear at an unlikely time and in an unlikely location. There will be eye contact and each of you will know. The chemistry will be overwhelming and you will say to yourself, *I know you.* Please don't let the person get away from you without speaking. He or she will think, *I know you*, also!

"Your soul mate has no idea why there is a connection until time has passed and information has been exchanged. And even then, it is not necessary to seek out past life regression. You will have a kinship that remains unexplained, yet spiritual and fulfilling.

"I found my soul mate, after all these years, just a few months ago at a psychic fair in Des Moines. William walked to my table and signed his name for a reading. When I looked in his eyes for the first time, there was something familiar about him. But I thought well, I see so many people - perhaps he's been here before. But it was his first visit. When he left the hotel, I knew I made a very big mistake to let him leave without personal words - such as, *I feel we have met before.*

"Of course, it isn't wise to try this in your local cocktail lounge. It definitely would be misunderstood coming from a man - or a woman these days. Such an old pick-up line! Does it still work?" she questioned.

We all laughed and I thought, *it probably does.*

"So, you may be thinking, '*how did she finally connect with William*'? It was by accident, but as you already know, there are no accidents. I was invited to a private home to teach past-life regression and William walked in the door as a guest. He participated in a regression and I took advantage of the opportunity to say, 'You know, the more I look at you, William, the more I have to admit - there's something very familiar about you.' "

A lady in the front row quickly asked, "What did he say?"

"William, would you like to tell her what you said?" Samantha asked sweetly and looked toward the back of the room.

All the heads turned. How would Samantha explain my answer?

"Sure, I don't mind. I said, 'well, maybe you finally remember something from a few months ago at the psychic fair.' "

A groan came from someone in the audience.

Only a professional like Samantha could have recovered as gracefully as she did.

"Not what you expected, my friends? Well it wasn't what I expected either. I was very disappointed. But then, I had no idea what had just happened to William in that room. Do you remember I said I was there for past-life regressions? Therein lies the answer.

"I was to find out later that William had seen *me* in his regression. I had been with him just minutes before in a deadly Indian massacre. He came out of his relaxation totally frightened and confused by what he'd seen. The Samantha he was looking at in the room was his wife who had been slaughtered in a past life.

"There were no words he could share with me at that time. But when we met again, we knew it was going to be forever - *and it will be.*

"Remember that it can happen to you today, next week, or five years from now. You just have to recognize it for what it is. Blessings abound in such a relationship as there is trust and caring, loyalty and even love."

"Are there any questions?"

Hands shot up all over the room and I took the opportunity to duck out the door and down to the lobby of the hotel. I picked an isolated area in the foyer so that no one would notice that my emotions had gotten the better of me.

CHAPTER TEN

I stayed at the fair the entire day, hoping to get time alone with Samantha, but she had clients waiting for readings until closing time. Her ability was far beyond my comprehension, and knew I had much to learn from this special woman who did not put herself in the limelight or boast of her accomplishments - her only interest was to help others.

When the readers and vendors began packing to leave the hotel, Samantha found me lingering in the doorway.

"William, you're still here."

"Yes, as a matter of fact, I am. You are one amazing woman. I came here to visit a friend for lunch and she turned out to be the hottest ticket in town."

"Are you proud of me?" she asked. "I'm proud of you, William. Your lecture was excellent."

"Thanks, but *yours* was much better! So, is there anything else you do that you haven't mentioned?"

"I think that's it," she laughed and reached for my arm. "Let's get out of here."

"But don't you have work to finish here?"

"Oh, no. Everyone takes care of his own area. I just have this one briefcase to carry back to the car. Seriously, William, your lecture was so well done. You should think about working with the people who come for help. You could do readings, you know."

"Me? I don't think so, Samantha. I'd be afraid I might give someone the wrong information."

"No, really. We should talk about that. Lets go downtown to this little place I know. We can just slip out quietly so we don't have any company. My people love to hang out and talk together after a weekend of psychic adventures."

We headed down the hall toward the stairs under the nearest exit sign, and I felt as if I were stealing the star of the show. It was a real high!

I pushed open the door for her and reached for her hand as I caught up with her on the stairs. Not a second later, Samantha stumbled and grabbed for me. Somehow we connected and I had her pinned against the handrail. Her eyes looked like a doe in the headlights. My heart was pounding.

"Samantha, are you OK? Here, sit on the steps for a minute."

She was gray. Her breathing was labored. She looked at me, but she didn't answer.

"Did you eat supper?" I asked. "You look terrible!"

"I guess that's the problem, William. Are you psychic, or what?"

She managed a smile. Samantha made me laugh all the time, but this one made me howl.

"Are you *nuts*? Sitting here on the steps like a little rag doll and still trying to make jokes. It doesn't take cosmic energy to solve this problem. I'm going to buy you the biggest steak we can find - and order it rare. Or, how about liver and onions? You look like you need some major iron."

"*YUCK!*" she squealed. "No way am I going to eat liver!"

"OK, then steak it is. I'm driving and you are leaving your Caravan here on the lot until tomorrow. I can take you home after dinner, and in the morning I'll drive you back to pick it up."

"That sounds perfect, William. I think I'm all right now."

I took her right hand in mine and slid my left arm behind her back. She was on her feet and stable, and the color had returned to her cheeks. I held on to her all the way to my car, and as I tightened the seat belt around her waist, I felt extremely emotional. I had finally given something of myself to a friend who had given so much to me.

a moment i will always treasure.

I chose a little place near the hotel with good food and a quiet atmosphere, and we settled at a candle-lit table for two toward the back of the room. She was pleased to note there was no liver on the menu, as she ordered filet mignon and a baked potato with butter. I ordered the same and we talked excitedly about the day while we sipped red wine and waited for our salads. Before long, Samantha brought the conversation around to how she could get me more involved in her work.

"As I said, William, you could do readings at the fairs."

"I don't think I want to do readings," I said. "I wouldn't want to give a person negative information when it came to me, and I would have a hard time charging for my work. What I really like is doing the deposessions with you. I studied healing also, and the combination of the two has been very rewarding. Why would you suggest I do readings?"

"For one thing, you aren't working at your office any more, and you could earn extra money. It's not deceptive to charge for your work because you have to live. You drive your car and you have expenses. It takes your time and effort and you should be paid something for those things. Plus, if they don't pay, they don't receive. There has to be an exchange in the Universe and that is very important - an exchange in energy. Money is just energy. It denotes energy someone spent. *'This is in payment for what I just gave - I am exchanging my energy for yours.'* "

"Samantha, I understand your conficence in my ability, but I feel that I do important work when I'm helping people connect with their loved ones. I like seeing them, relaying messages and giving truth. Maybe I could just continue to lecture at the fairs."

"That's an excellent idea, William, and it will be a good source for clientele. Your lectures will reflect your skill and the people will come to you for help. I can see a business right in your own home in no time at all. What would your wife think about that?"

"Julia is incapable of judging anything for what it is, at this point. She exists in a world of her own and doesn't care what I do or what goes on in the house. When you came to help me that night, she was dead drunk in her room, as usual, and didn't know or care what was going on. I could have an entire room addition built and she wouldn't see it!"

"That's almost funny, if it wasn't so pitiful, William. However, a computer area would not necessitate a room addition."

"I was just joking about that."

"I can send people to you if you wish. You know my business connections are all over the United States, and at this point, you can see it's more than I can handle. When I got into this, I gave free readings at the ladies' auxiliaries and men's clubs in the area, so you could do the same with lectures. There are a lot of people who would come to you for help - you just have to reach out for them.

"Remember though, there is no harm in charging for your work - say $40 a session to start and then move to $60, like we do with our depossessions. Your expenses continue to mount. Julia should not have to be the bread-winner in your home, no matter how much you have saved in the bank."

The dinner was as satisfying as our conversation, and I left the restaurant with the feeling that my life could get no better. Samantha thanked me for the evening and said the food was exactly what she needed. I told her that's what soul mates do for each other and she said,

"I owe you one."

I took a longer route on our return drive to Des Moines because I hated to see our conversation come to an end. We never seemed to run out of words, and more often than not, I knew what she was about to say even before she said it. As I rounded a turn near her home, I saw - *fire*!

Samantha saw it at the same instant. Flames were shooting out of the fireplace chimney of a mobile home on the right side of the road. I slammed on the brakes and we each bolted out of our doors to run instinctively for the home. I pulled on the trailer door handle and it came open easily.

"*You have a chimney fire!*" I yelled, as I rushed

inside. Samantha was on my heels and nearly tripped on the owner's dog as it ran past her into the night.

I continued to shout, "*Your trailer's on fire! You have a chimney fire!*"

A woman came rushing from a back bedroom and grabbed her telephone to call 911. Her little girl was right behind her, trying to hold on to her mother's pant leg.

"*I need some salt!*" I yelled to her, and she ran for the cabinets as she punched in the numbers.

Samantha moved quickly to pick up the child.

"My kitty!" the little one cried. She tried to pull out of Samantha's arms to get to the calico cat that had just streaked across the living room.

Samantha caught the cat by the scruff of its neck as it clawed its way to the top of a sofa, and they were out the front door in seconds.

I salted the flames at the base of the fireplace and the woman and I ran for the front yard. We were surprised that the fire truck was already in view. Samantha had put the cat in my car and she was in the passenger seat holding the little girl on her lap. The child was totally upset until she saw her mother and me coming toward her.

When the firemen had the situation under control, we were free to continue on our way. Samantha and I were elated. We had turned that corner at the instant we were needed. We sat in the car in front of her house talking excitedly about the rescue.

"Samantha, we worked as a team. It was so natural. We both knew exactly what to do without saying a word to each other."

"Yes, we did. It was perfect. So now you must believe what I've been telling you all along - we had to have done this work many times before. There is not a doubt in my mind that we are supposed to work together."

I reluctantly walked Samantha to her door, but I left knowing I would see her the next day for a series of depossessions and lunch. We decided we would try a Chinese restaurant that recently opened in the area, although I was not sure I would like Samantha's menu suggestion of egg fu yung. She said she needed more protein in her diet and decided that since it would be good for her, it would be good for me. I wasn't so sure about that.

CHAPTER ELEVEN

Over the weekend, I decided to enlist the services of my son and update my computer. He was delighted that his dad seemed to have an interest in getting back to reality and returning to work. The delight faded within minutes of his stepping into my living room.

"You want to do *WHAT?*"

"Now wait a minute, Mark. You never *did* relate to psychology, so don't let metaphysics throw you over the edge. I have an entirely different outlook on life - have had it ever since I got out of the hospital. I'd appreciate it if you would just work with me on this and help me get my computer on line so I can move ahead with my projects."

"But Dad, this is foolish. Dr. Vargas has nearly doubled his workload covering for you. You have to call him and tell him what's up. And while you're at it, explain it to me!"

"Nothing to explain, Mark. I choose to work with Samantha at this point in time, and I can't say what will happen in the future. She is confident in my ability and she'll be sending people to me as soon as I get set up. And where it goes from there, I can't say. I only know what I feel and it feels right to me."

"What about Mom? Are you seeing this woman on a personal level? Are you planning to leave my mother?"

"This has nothing to do with your mother. This has to do with me. Samantha and I have a working relationship - almost like a partnership. We work extremely well together and have been helping people from all over the United States with physical and mental problems. She told me I can build up my own base here at home with people she refers, and I know it's what I want to do. I want you to meet her, Mark. And, trust me, there is nothing going on between us."

"I know you will tell me this is none of my business, but you know Mom is in a fragile state. Why can't you and Samantha help *her*?"

"Julia has to make her choices, and she chooses to continue on as she is. I know that sounds lame to you, but it comes right down to the fact that it's her decision. Perhaps one day a change will come."

"I guess nothing I say will make a you change your mind?"

"No," I answered firmly.

"All right then, Dad. This will take a few days, but I'll do what I can to help you. Your computer is outdated, you know, so maybe we should just go shopping. We can buy you all the bells and whistles you need to get in business. But first, I think we should call Samantha and ask what types of programs she uses so you can both be on the same page. Then you will be all set to start *whatever-it-is* you do. You aren't going to practice on *me*, are you?"

"I'm ready any time you want to start," I laughed.

He laughed too, and we hugged. He felt rigid against my arms, but I knew it was a natural reaction. Soon he would feel as comfortable as I had become with an embrace.

Julia wandered in and out of the room over the weekend to see what we were doing. I explained it to her and told her about my business partnership with the psychic, Samantha.

"William, this makes no sense. What do you think you're doing? This Samantha chick - who the hell does she think she is, giving you all these ideas? You have a decent, respectable job, and you have to call Dr. Vargas and tell him he can leave because you are coming back to work!"

Just that quickly, she forgot her train of thought, lit another cigarette and turned to Mark.

"So, how's Nicholas? What was it - first grade he just finished?"

"Sure, Mom. You know it was first grade."

"Well, he needs to come over and spend summer vacation with his grandpa who's on a *FOREVER* vacation - doing *CRAP* since he went insane in that hospital!"

She threw back her head and left the room with a hiss and a decisive puff of cigarette smoke. Mark looked at me and I looked at him. There was nothing to be said.

On Friday of the next week, I called Samantha. I was as wired as my office!

"Good morning," I said politely, "this is William speaking."

"Oh, you sound so business-like," she said. "Can I come over and see your new office?"

"Do you have an appointment?"

"What time do you have available?"

"Hmmm...let me check my book. I have an opening in 10 minutes. Can you be here by 11:18?"

"I'm on my way."

I met her at the door at 11:17 and she was ecstatic. She threw her arms around me for only an instant and said, "Show me!"

I led her down the hall to the spare room I used as an office, but it was nothing in comparison to her work area. Mine looked sterile with rows of bound texts in a glass-fronted bookcase, a dark oak desk converted to a computer table, and my brown leather office chair. The green tinted-glass office lamp would have to be the first thing to hit the trash.

"I know I have to make some adjustments, Samantha, but Mark will help me with that. I never did spend much time in here, you know. I made business phone calls and used a few of the reference books."

"It's so nice, William. Can I stay a few hours and show you how to set up some data bases?"

"I knew you'd say that. I'll get another chair. How about a glass of iced water with a slice of lemon?"

I turned on the stereo in the living room on the way back to my office and brought her drink and a chair. We worked for hours and were surprised to see how much time had passed. She was an excellent teacher in every respect. I took notes and wished I had taken more classes in programming. She assured me it would come more easily with practice, and I trusted her on that score.

Then we did simple things, like sending a message to her office and putting an outgoing message on my answering machine. She left just before Julia was to return from summer school, even though she insisted on meeting my wife. I told her about Julia's hostility and suggested we wait a little while longer for an introduction.

Before long, the answering machine was full of inquiries, and not all of them came through Samantha. People were telling their friends about their past-life regressions and how they were helped by the experience.

One health problem concerned an allergic reaction to cats. When the woman was regressed, she found the source of the problem and I suggested she leave the problem in the past where it belonged. Regressions were also instrumental in curing phobias and bad habits that were difficult to overcome.

I remember a woman who had gotten my name from Samantha. She was a hearing-impaired nurse and she had a son who was deaf. She taught her son to read lips and thought she had done the right thing, but he was having a lot of trouble in school. I decided to write notes to him through my computer, and he wrote notes to me to say he was frightened because he could not always see the lips of the other children. He thought they were making fun of him.

This time I used my psychology and encouraged the mother to enroll him in a school for the deaf. He could learn sign language and be with other children with similar problems. I did not get feedback on this child's progress, but I suspect there was improvement if his mother decided to take my advice.

My meditation classes also formed just as Rodney's had - accidentally. They grew by word-of-mouth. But as in other things, the bad came with the good. Samantha sent a bizarre gentleman to my house who told me he knew all about psychics and tricks they used. Then he asked for advise and pleaded to be a part of one of my classes. It was difficult to get him to leave. The next day when I complained to Samantha over lunch, she said,

"I didn't know how to get rid of him, so I sent him to you."

We laughed. The situation got more hysterical

after she told me she figured it would be easier to get him out of her house if she gave him my address, as well as my phone number. We settled down, but we were laughing again within minutes. Our times together were always wonderful and the stories and laughter kept us at lunch for hours. It was important for me to get my calls and office work completed in the morning because my afternoons were shot. Lunches with Samantha were the highlight of my days.

"William," she said, "when are you going to admit that you are the best? You're so much better than I am. I see symbols in the messages I receive, but you get the whole story - like a movie, complete with color, lights and surround sound. I still believe you should be doing readings at the fairs right along with your lectures."

"I'm doing fine just being there with the people. Remember, I helped a woman at the last fair because I knew there was something wrong back at home with her daughter's baby? I knew it the moment I saw her walk into the room. As far as I'm concerned, that's the most rewarding work in the world."

"You were right on track, William. She was so grateful for your help and came back later to say they took her granddaughter to the hospital with dehydration and fever. You know, you saved another life."

"I guess I never really thought about it that way."

"You must realize your gift, William. I'm going to a psychic conference in Indiana for three days next week, and I want you to come with me. You'd have to talk it over with Julia, of course."

"You know my relationship with Julia; it wouldn't matter to her in the least. But I told my grandson he could spend some time with me, and we have plans to do some fishing. He'd be very disappointed if I backed out of the deal."

"You'll have so much fun with him, William. I understand how you feel. I have a grandson named Adam. He's going to be eight this year."

"Really? You never talk about your family."

"My daughter Sarah lives in Montana and she doesn't get to bring Adam to see me very often. How about calling me when Nicholas visits you so I can come over and meet him?"

"That would be great. The two of you will get along fine. He has his share of *woo woo*."

"*Woo-woo*? Is that what I think it is?"

"Sure is. He's pretty gifted for a little kid. I always thought he had an over-active imagination, but now I understand. I gave him that code word so he knows when it's all right to tell what he's getting. I tell him he's special and that a lot of children his age can't see what he sees, so he shouldn't share it with the kids at school. Now he quietly asks me every time a client comes here, 'is he a *woo-woo*?' "

"I can see that Nicholas and I will be great friends," laughed Samantha.

Great friends, indeed! Samantha ended up spending more time with Nicholas than I did. I was busy at my computer one afternoon a few weeks later, and I heard them talking and laughing in the kitchen.

"What's going on?" I asked, as I rounded the corner.

"Grandpa, look what I can do!" said Nicholas excitedly. Samantha has these cards face down and I can tell her what they are before she turns them over."

"That's excellent. How do you do it?"

"I don't know, but watch me."

Samantha showed Nicholas 6 new cards. Then she shuffled the cards and placed 5 of them up and one down. She pointed to the one facedown.

"What is this?" she asked.

"A red four!" he yelped.

"Right! You got it right!" I said, and I hugged him from around the back of his chair.

"I can do it the other way too," he chirped.

"What other way?" I asked.

"Samantha puts them all face-down and I know what they are!"

"He's a sharp little kid, William," Samantha said, as she laid out more cards.

It was the most intriguing thing. She played the game over and over with him and told me later that she put in new cards to test him and he called each one correctly. He didn't realize it was a test. To him, it was a wonderful game.

When she left that day, she suggested I let him guess who was calling when the phone rang. When he was correct, I was to give him a nickel or a dime. If he was wrong, I was to say he could try again the next time. It was one more way to improve his mind.

Nicholas loved music, so he had my stereo blasting all the time. It never mattered what kind of music he found, just so it was music. One morning, Samantha paid me a surprise visit and asked me to come out to the car with her. She had brought along something special for Nicholas - an old portable keyboard.

"He's going to flip when he sees this, Samantha. Where did you get it?"

"I used to play piano in a band. I sang with them too, but I refuse to tell you how long ago."

"Really? Wonders never cease! Let's hook it up. Mark's bringing Nicholas over in a little while."

We put the keyboard in a small bedroom adjacent to my office, and Samantha played a few tunes for me. I was never interested in playing an instrument, but I had a sizable collection of recorded pop music.

"Sing for me, Samantha," I said.

"No, I can't. I haven't for years."

"Doesn't matter. If you can play like that, you can just sing along. I won't critique you because I can't sing a note."

Samantha turned on the bench and looked up at me.

"What's wrong?" I asked.

"I don't have the breath I had back then. You can give me back my music, but you can't restore my breath."

"Samantha, let me look at you."

I relaxed quickly and concentrated on her body.

"Samantha, you had a lung removed...on the right side!"

"You scanned me, didn't you. I see I can't get away with anything around you. I had lung cancer three years ago and the only choice was surgery and chemotherapy."

"Have you been back to the doctor recently? I get a sense that you should call him."

"What else do you see, William? I *have* to know what you see."

"I see dark spots on the other lung. But I don't see a problem anywhere else in your body."

"I've been taking a lot of vitamins since my surgery, and I'm taking kelation treatments. It has to be working because I feel better."

"Why won't you believe what I see, Samantha? You believe what I see when we work together, so you have to believe me now."

"I don't *want* to believe it."

"I'll go to the doctor with you. You need X-rays and an MRI, or whatever it takes, and you need it soon. Don't be afraid. I won't let anything happen to you."

The doorbell interrupted us and I had to leave her to open the front door for Nicholas. I should have had five more minutes to comfort Samantha, or to convince her to call her doctor from my phone. But Nicholas stormed her when I told him she was waiting for him with a surprise, and the moment was lost.

They spent the entire morning pounding on the keyboard as I worked in my study. It was good for both of them to laugh and play. It was good for my heart as well. Around noon, Samantha ducked in to see me and suggested that all three of us go out to lunch - her treat.

"William, before we leave, come in and see Nicholas for a minute. He's going to play some notes for you."

"Grandpa, watch me!" Nicholas yelled.

Samantha stood behind Nicholas and began to call notes. Nicholas found each one. Then she winked at me and opened her mouth to call a note. She moved her lips to say *D-flat* without uttering the sound, and Nicholas reached out and hit D-flat. He looked up at her and smiled.

"You were going to tell me D-flat, weren't you?" he said, innocently.

"You bet I was!"

"Nicholas, that was wonderful," I laughed. "I'll bet you already know where we're going for lunch."

All too soon, Julia's obligations at summer school were over, as were Samantha's visits. I missed having her in my home. I missed the work and the laughter and the music.

Nicholas left for South Carolina with his mom and dad to enjoy the ocean, and that left Julia and I alone once again. We were like strangers after all the years of separation due to work schedules and alcohol. It was evident from the first day that our conversations would be limited to sarcasm. I came to the conclusion that our relationship could not withstand much more.

CHAPTER TWELVE

Despite Julia's objections, I continued working with Samantha at her home as often as she needed me for deposessions. We always made sure the work included at least a two-hour lunch. Unfortunately, I could not get Samantha to cooperate with me and call her doctor. When I noticed her gray complexion or shortness of breath, she passed it off as having had a stressful, tiring day, and insisted that vitamins and kelation were all she needed. I suppose my emotion and my heart got the best of me, and I decided it was time to make another major decision in my life. I wanted to be more than just Samantha's friend and co-worker.

I was extremely nervous one day when we returned from lunch, and she picked up on it immediately. She gave me one of those looks, and I decided she already knew what I was going to say.

"Samantha, I'm going to leave Julia. It's impossible for me to continue to live like this, and I can't stay in that house."

"Oh no, please. That's a very serious thing to consider. If it has anything to do with your feelings for me, you must reconsider. You must stay with Julia."

I could see the fear in her face as she went on.

"There's not enough time for us, William. I asked the guides and they told me we can never be together in this lifetime. But they assured me that you are the soul mate who will be with me forever. In fact, we are *twin souls*."

"I never heard *that* expression."

"It's one soul that decides it can learn more quickly and advance by breaking in half to form twin souls. That is what happened with us a long time ago. You can feel my pain as I feel yours."

"I have trouble catching my breath sometimes coming up the basement stairs, but I think nothing of it. I'm sure it's an after-effect of the flu. I don't want you to worry any more, Samantha. I can work on you and make you well."

"You can try healing energy, but if it doesn't work, you can't take on the guilt. I know how you are, William."

"I'm going to do everything I can to help you, Samantha. You're too important to me. And no matter what happens, I'm still leaving Julia. I can't live that lie any more."

"Please, William, it's important that you stay with Julia. I'm going to fix it. I can't explain it, but I'm going to fix it."

"I don't understand what you mean. If you die, we can't be together."

I didn't want to leave her that day. In fact, I didn't remember the drive back to my house. My Samantha knew the truth of her illness and had known for some time. I walked around my house that evening feeling lifeless. Julia was down for the night. I tried to work, but I couldn't. I tried to sleep and that didn't work either. I wished it could be my problem - not hers. She was the best gift I was ever given and she was going to be taken from me.

I had members of every meditation group in the area working on Samantha, and I was trying my best to keep feeding her my own healing energy. I entered her name on the Universal Healing web site. I knew we could help her if we all worked together.

One night my phone rang at 3:00 a.m.

"You have to come here right now!"

samantha!

I threw on some clothes and raced over to her house. The door was open and I took two porch steps at a time.

"William," she said, as she forced a smile, "look at your clothes."

so, nothing matches...why did you...

Samantha's face was gray and she was grimacing in pain. I ran to the couch and scooped her up in my arms - it felt as if she weighed nothing.

"You are going to the emergency room!"

I lowered her gently into the passenger seat of my car and attached the seat belt. It took all I had to keep from crying.

The drive was excruciating. Samantha insisted she had to go to Mary Greeley Medical Center in Ames where she had been treated in the past. Greeley Center was 30 miles north, and I was afraid she would die right in my car if I drove that far. She told me there was a note in her appointment book that I had to find if anything happened to her. I promised I would find it.

I waited in the family lounge for hours until a nurse came to find me.

"Are you William?"

"Yes, I am. How is she?"

"She's in intensive care and she's insisting on see-ing you. I don't think she will calm down until we bring you in. Are you a relative?"

"No, I'm a friend."

"Well, it looks like we'll have to make an exception to the rule in this case. She's hysterical and not reacting to the drugs."

As soon as Samantha saw me, she stopped crying and she reached for my hand. She was asleep in a matter of minutes. By nine that morning, she was admitted and moved to Oncology on the fifth floor for tests. I knew I could not leave her there alone. I stayed all the next day and through the weekend, not caring about anyone or anything outside of that room.

Samantha's MRI and blood tests verified our fears. An aggressive malignant tumor was found in her left lung. She was put on a schedule of radiation therapy which would total 20 treatments. Chemotherapy was also prescribed and appointments were scheduled to begin within a few days back at our Des Moines health facility, Mercy West.

Of course I insisted on driving her for chemo and radiation every morning, and I decided to make it more pleasant by planning either breakfast on the way or lunch on the return. Her appetite was terrible, but she remained cheerful and hopeful, even though she knew the prognosis was not good.

Samantha began feeding me information as if there was so much to tell and she had no time. She insisted that I learn to operate her computer web site and she showed me all the records. We worked with her clients as the requests appeared and stopped whenever she was tired. It was obvious she wasn't herself when she didn't resist my move to cancel her in-home appointments.

One day on the way home from chemo, Samantha told me some personal things about her former marriage, her family life, her daughter and her grandson. They were memories she felt she needed to share and I was grateful for every word. But then she nearly broke my heart when she gave me her daughter's telephone number in Montana and told me to be sure to call if she became severely ill. I promised her everything, but in my heart I felt I would not survive if she were not allowed to live.

Even though I knew Samantha needed a lot of rest to regain her strength, it hurt me to leave each afternoon. I told her to call me any time, and I assured her I would return each morning, even after the treatments ended.

My Julia didn't know or care where I was. Now that she was on her summer break, she could drink all day...her idea of paradise. I soon discovered that a quiet house had its advantages, so I worked every evening on information I forwarded from Samantha's computer. I was able to keep up with her clients as well as my own. Exhaustion would hit me just after midnight.

I can't say I remember having a problem sleeping, but as the nights went on, I awoke several times feeling that I should check on Samantha. It seemed foolish. Was she trying mental telepathy? I decided to play her game.

"Samantha, did I wake you?"

"William, I was thinking of you and you called."

"Oh, my gosh! I just knew it! So, how long have you been doing this?"

"Thinking of you?"

"No, how long have you been trying to get me to call you?"

"I wasn't trying to get you to call me, honestly. I

just woke up and started thinking about you, and I guess you picked up the message. That's neat!"

"Sure is! We could have these useless telephones disconnected and save some cash. Let's practice this during the day, though. You're supposed to be getting some sleep so you get well."

"OK," she laughed, and she hung up.

Over the weekend, I was shopping with Mark and Nicholas for school supplies. It was hard to believe the summer was slipping by so quickly. The second grade teacher had sent a list to each child in the class and we decided to have a boys' day out. I was in charge of the cart, Mark was reading the list, and Nicholas was running down the aisles to pick up his treasures.

It came on suddenly - the fingers of my left hand started to tingle, and within a minute or so, my hand was bright red. I let go of the cart handle and shook my arm. I could feel my blood pressure rise instantly. I was scared to death!

"Dad, what's wrong with your hand?" asked Mark, startled.

"I haven't the slightest idea! I don't know what's happening!"

The flush went up my arm and seemed to pick up a purple hue. I sat down on the floor against a shelf of book bags. There was no pain, just warmth and that ridiculous color. Nicholas turned immediately, as if he sensed a problem, and ran to sit cross-legged next to me.

"Grandpa! Wow! Look at your arm! Does it hurt?"

"No, but it looks as bright as one of your cherry Popsicles, doesn't it? I don't remember bumping my hand on anything."

Just as quickly as it started, it stopped. Mark and Nicholas stared in disbelief.

"Well, I'll be darn," said Mark. "Look at that. The color is almost back to normal. Does it feel better now?"

"Never did feel bad...just a tingle in my fingers and then, *WHAM*."

Nicholas got up and said, "Ok, let's go get some more stuff for school."

Mark and I laughed at a second-grader's lack of concern, and then realized that I was perfectly all right. We continued on with our shopping, but not before Mark gave me exactly what I expected - advise about seeing a doctor. He dropped me at home about four and I went right to the phone.

"Samantha? Hi! How are your feeling?"

"Hi, William. I feel pretty good today...getting ready to eat dinner. What's going on?"

"Listen, I was just out shopping with my boys, and I have to ask you a strange question."

"What?"

"Did you do anything to my hand this afternoon?"

"Your hand? I don't know."

"Were you trying to send me a message today?"

"I was trying telepathy again, but I don't know how I could have done something to your hand."

"I'm going to hang up now, but I want you to give me five minutes, and then I want you to do that telepathy thing again, OK?"

"OK."

I took off my watch and ring, sat down on my bed and looked at my left hand. Five minutes went by...seven minutes...

this is crazy.

Suddenly it felt as though someone had stabbed my fingers! The sensation ran up my hand as I grabbed the telephone.

"Samantha, did you do it?" I asked excitedly.

"*YES!*" she screamed in my ear. "Let's try it again!"

She got through to me within minutes. We were laughing so hard I had to bury my face in my pillow.

"Samantha this is unbelievable. We're so much in tune. How about stopping now and experimenting more tomorrow, OK? You need to get yourself in bed so you get strong."

"How do you expect me to sleep after all this?" she asked, choking back the laughter.

"Don't think so much! *Neither* of us will get any sleep if you lie there and think about me. I'll see you in the morning. Sweet dreams."

Samantha and I couldn't wait to get started working with our new mode of communication. Her session at the clinic felt like an eternity, and we were still giggling as we slid into the booth of the Chinese restaurant off Douglas Avenue.

"Ready?" she laughed.

"Hit me."

Samantha closed her eyes. I stared at my hand.

...Nothing.

We waited ten minutes and gave up. After egg fu yung - her version of a protein rush - I drove to a nearby park so we could try another experiment. I walked down to the lake and sat on the bench while she sat in my car and tried to send me something.

"Think harder!" I screamed up the hill.

I could hear her laughter from there. We gave up after half an hour and fed our fortune cookies to the ducks. The solution, we decided, was that we needed more distance between us. Why use telepathy when we were within earshot?

CHAPTER THIRTEEN

The time came for Samantha to check back into the hospital in Ames and have blood work and more X-rays to check her progress, so I drove her once again to Mary Greely Medical Center. She asked me to wait a few days to visit until her tests were completed, because she would be in and out of her room with appointments. My hand turned colors several times during that time period and I assumed she needed help. So, I sent healing energy back to her. On the morning of the third day, my hand hurt to the point of waking me out of a sound sleep. I dialed her hospital room immediately.

"It took you five minutes!" Samantha laughed. Look out the window, William. Isn't this a magnificent sunrise?"

"You crazy woman. I don't see anything magnificent about it. It's raining down here in Des Moines! But I don't think you woke me up to tell me that. You must have some really good news. How did the tests come out?"

"Don't know. I have one more today. They're putting a scope down my throat for a biopsy and I'm so afraid something will go wrong. I gave your number to the doctor, just in case."

"I'll come tomorrow."

"No, tomorrow's Saturday. You need to spend time with your family because Nicholas starts school after the weekend. I get out on Monday, so do you think you could pick me up in the morning?"

"I'll be there, Samantha. You know you got through

to me a few times with the hand trick."

"I was thinking about you all the time, William. I'm surprised you didn't end up in the emergency room with a fluorescent arm."

We laughed at ourselves, and I decided at that moment I would go on Saturday and surprise her. My heart was aching for her, as was my body. She had no idea that the tests were hard on me also. I could feel her pain.

When I walked into her room, the look on her face told me everything I needed to know.

"Oh, William, you're *here*! Come and hold my hand!"

"I couldn't wait until Monday…I miss you so much," I confessed.

I sat on the edge of her bed and took her hand in mine, resisting the urge to lean over to kiss her.

"You sound hoarse, Samantha. I guess it's from the biopsy."

"I think so, William. I'm supposed to have Jell-O and tea today, but I'm really hungry. Can you go get me something in the cafeteria?"

"They have some things to eat in the lobby area. It's a combination gift shop and snack shop. I'll go see what looks good, but I'll have to sneak it in to you. What if I get caught feeding you solid food and they kick me out of here?"

"If you go, I go!" she laughed.

The gift/snack area was unusual, to say the least. It had small, square 1950's tables with chrome chairs, and walls lined with teddy bears and floral arrangements. I surveyed a glass case of desserts and chose what looked the best - a slice of carrot cake, covered securely in plastic wrap. I paid the volunteer, hid the cake under my jacket like a common criminal and hit the elevator button.

"Oh, my favorite!" she laughed, as I delivered the bounty.

"The wrapper crinkles," I whispered. "Open it under the cover so the nurse doesn't hear the plastic wrap."

"Stand in front of mc," Samantha laughed, "so she can't see what we're doing. Do you want a bite?"

"No, darn it. Just eat it quick before we both get thrown out."

We joked the entire afternoon. She was jealous of the woman in the next bed who caught my attention and began a conversation with me. I guess it hit me when she coyly asked me to sit in the chair on the other side of her bed. I was encouraged and delighted, but all too soon it was time to go.

"Are you coming back tomorrow?" she asked, as she forced a pout onto her lips.

"Do you want me to?"

"Yes!" she brightened. "And, will you bring me my lunch? I mean, just in case they are still fooling around with this dumb diet."

"Sure. How about a picnic lunch with chicken salad and something sweet for dessert?"

"Like what?" Samantha grinned. "Carrot cake?"

Sunday didn't come fast enough for me. I stopped at the supermarket near my house to pick up chicken salad from the deli and croissants from the bakery. Oh, and half a carrot cake! Then I found bright blue paper plates and a package of yellow forks and knives. As I was turning to leave the party aisle, I spotted the perfect candleholder. It had a sunshine on one side and a rainbow on the other.

My "picnic basket" was a pair of plastic carryout bags, but Samantha didn't even notice. She was so happy to see me, and she invited her roommate, Maggie, to join us. I pulled over some chairs and opened my packages, watching the delight in Samantha's eyes. She laughed over the carrot cake and cried over the candleholder.

"No one ever made me a picnic lunch, William. I wish we could do this again when I get out of here. Maybe we could go back to the park?"

"Great idea. Did the doctor say you could go home tomorrow?"

"Yes, I can leave at ten. Maggie gets to leave tomorrow, too...don't you, Mag." She smiled and turned to her roommate. I looked at her too and suddenly saw something.

"Maggie," I said, "I don't know where you live, but I see an accident at a highway exit ramp. There's a sign that says, *Randall*."

"You must be joking," chuckled Maggie. "Samantha must have told you where I live and you two are trying to give me the *heebie-jeebies*."

"No, Mag. I didn't tell him any such thing," Samantha insisted. "Trust me If he sees it, he knows."

"I do take Highway 35, of course," said Maggie, "but I can take a different exit. This is scaring me. Do you really see something at Randall?"

"Yes, I really do. I think it would be wise for you to avoid that intersection at all cost tomorrow, and for the next few days. It may be that an accident will occur between two other cars and your car will become tangled in the wreckage. You should take the other route."

"I've never gotten information like this from any-one, but I don't intend to risk my life just to prove you wrong. There are several other roads I can take. Thanks so much, William. Samantha's a lucky woman to have you."

"I *am* a lucky woman, Maggie, but we're not a cou-ple. He's married and we just work together."

"Well, whatever you two have, it's special."

Samantha and I took a leisurely drive on our return to Des Moines the next morning. It was wonderful to have her all to myself again. The doctor called in her pre-scriptions, so we stopped at the pharmacy. Then I sur-prised her by stopping at the park. We sat at the lake for a while and watched the ducks. Her color was good and the new medications she was given in the hospital were work-ing wonders for her breathing. I told her about the clients who left messages while she was away, but I hadn't asked her the test results, and she had not volunteered informa-tion. This was not a good sign. I put my arm around her shoulder.

"Tell me what the doctor said," I asked, gently.

"It isn't good."

My heart sank. I could feel my head getting light. I could feel her weakness, her disappointment, her emo-tion.

"We can't give up hope, Samantha. We'll work harder; we'll try to get a lung transplant, if that's what it takes."

"The doctor said my cancer has spread to my bones, William. I can take another round of chemo, but no more radiation. He told me the chemo would just prolong the inevitable."

"Oh, no! I can't lose you, Samantha."

I pulled her to me on the bench and lost my composure. She and I cried until we had no more tears. We sat holding each other for a long time and then walked slowly back up the hill to my car. The silence was deafening. I drove her home and carried her suitcase into her room. She sat on the couch and motioned for me to sit beside her.

"William, I'd like to go to Montana and visit my daughter and grandson. I'm afraid I won't get another chance to see them."

"You can't go that far alone," I insisted.

"I think I can. You and Nicholas showed me something I missed by not having Adam with me. Your grandson is so special and I want to feel that too. I didn't realize how important family could be until now. Sarah and I need time, too. She moved from here when Adam was three and I miss her so much."

"I want to take you there, Samantha," I said, as I reached for her hand. Tears welled in my eyes.

"Can you do that? Can you get away?"

"*Can* I? Nothing will stop me."

"I know Sarah will love you, William. And do you think we can take Nicholas with us? He and Adam would have great fun."

"I'll see what I can do about that. I'll take care of everything, OK?"

"OK. One more thing...I want you to take my house key with you."

"All right."

Samantha had given up. I just knew it, and it was killing me. I wanted to call her doctor and curse him for his negative diagnosis. She wasn't going to die and I planned to make sure of that.

I stopped in to see her every morning as usual and did all I could think of to keep the positive energy flowing. She was feeling pretty well, actually, and we worked together when the calls came in. Samantha was brilliant; every day was special.

"William, Mrs. Mathison just called from Arkansas. She's been calling me for years for personal readings, and she had an Alzheimer patient wander away yesterday afternoon."

"Is she a doctor?"

"No, she's a nursing home administrator - a real nice lady. She called the authorities but the search party hasn't found him. There was heavy rain and lightning overnight and the dogs couldn't pick up his scent in the storm."

"Are you getting anything on it?"

"I need a minute."

Samantha sat in one of her black leather armchairs and closed her eyes. I sat in the other chair watching her and realized I was smiling. Of course she's getting something! What a dumb question.

She knew the man's name and the location of the nursing home in Fayetteville, Arkansas. In a matter of seconds, her body relaxed and she was there. She was seeking life for a stranger even though she was losing her own. I can't explain the respect I felt at that moment.

A few more minutes went by. Samantha opened her eyes and went to the telephone. Her face was expressionless as she walked past me. I was eager to hear the conversation.

"I have to talk to Mildred Mathison," she said quietly. "Tell her Samantha has the information she requested."

There was silence.

"Mildred, this is Samantha. I'm going to give you a series of symbols I received from my guides. Do you have a pencil and paper?

"Write this down: ...Missouri, owl, woods, school, acorn, rural mailboxes, church, construction and bus. You'll find him alive."

Samantha hung up the phone softly and sat quietly at her workstation, still reflecting on the moment. Then she turned to me and smiled.

Later that evening I was at home finishing some work on the computer. The phone rang about 10:30.

"William, it's Samantha. I have good news! Mildred just called and she said her Alzheimer resident was found."

"I had no doubt, Samantha. Tell me what she said."

"Well, she took my message to the Sheriff, but he just smiled and handed it right back to her. She was livid. She went back to the home, rounded up some attendants, and they headed out to look for him on their own with my list of clues."

"And?"

"And, it took a while, she said, but they found him alive. She called an ambulance and he was transported to an emergency room in Fayetteville. He had some scratches and about thirty ticks, but he's back at the nursing home now and doing all right."

"Tell me where they found him, Samantha. You're

making me crazy!"

"He was in the woods along Old Missouri Road, across the street from a church that's under construction. A rural mailbox was on the road, directly in the path of where he was found. He was about fifteen feet from a large oak, and Mildred said she could see the grade school and a yellow school bus when she looked north through the trees. I couldn't wait to call you, William. I'm thrilled!"

"And you said you *only see symbols*. Just look at what a gift you gave that gentleman with your symbols. I'm so proud of you and the work you do for all your people, and I love you for making me a part of your world."

"What a sweet thing to say, William. We have lots more to do, don't we? I need you to help me for as long as I'm here - and then it's going to be all yours. I trust you to carry on for me."

"Don't say that! You're not going to leave me and I don't want to hear any more about it. You get some sleep and I'll see you in the morning, OK?"

"OK."

CHAPTER FOURTEEN

Mark called me to say he and Kate were planning a seventh birthday party for Nicholas the next Sunday. I decided to check with Julia.

"His seventh?" she said, as she lit a cigarette. "Already? Didn't we just do that?"

"A year ago - when he was *six*," I snapped.

"I don't go out on Sundays. I don't even go out on Saturdays, for that matter. And, while we're on the subject, where the heck do you go every weekend?"

"I'm *here* every weekend, Julia! You're the one who's *OUT*."

"Oh, aren't you the smart ass. You and your little girlfriend Samantha, playing house! No wonder I drink!"

"Good try, Julia. You want to blame me for what you've been doing for the past nine years. You've been drinking straight vodka since Mark left home.

"Give me one good reason why should I quit drinking. For you? You're not a husband to me any more! You haven't touched me in years!"

"What are you saying? Do you think I'm having an affair with Samantha?"

"*YES!*"

"Well, you're *WRONG!*"

"Am I? No, you're the one with the problem here, bud! And you better straighten up your act and get back to work or I'll get a lawyer and kick your butt right out of here. Then see if your little Sammy-girl will support you!"

She stepped up defiantly and blew a puff of smoke in my face. Then she swirled the ice in her glass and stamped out of the room.

I fell into a kitchen chair in shock. The drunk whipped me. She was not as oblivious to what was going on around her as I thought. But she was dead wrong about me having an affair. I couldn't deny my feelings for Samantha, but no one could accuse me of more. Did it look bad to anyone else? Did I care? I called Mark.

"Yah, Dad, what's up?"

"I'm calling about the birthday party for Nicholas. What does he want to do?"

"We're having a picnic at the park. Nicholas is so excited. He's going to take his fishing pole cause he figures you'll bring yours. What do you think?"

"That's pretty cute, Mark. Sounds like a plan. Your mother's taking a pass on it, though. She said she already has plans, but she'll send along a gift."

"I get it. You don't have to say any more, Dad. We all plan to meet at the park about noon for lunch. Kate's bringing sandwiches from the deli and we ordered the cake - chocolate, of course."

"Is Nicholas around? I'd like to tell him I'm coming to his party."

"Sure, hold on."

"Hi, Grandpa! Are you coming to my birthday party? Are you bringing your fishing pole?"

"Yup! Wanna dig some worms before we go?"

"Oh, wow! I can go Saturday after cartoons. Do you know I'm going to be seven?"

"I sure do, Nicholas. And you're my very favorite special boy."

"Hey, that sounds like what Samantha says. Can she come too?"

"I'll call and see. I think she'd like that. Now run along and I'll see you on Saturday. You bring your old sand bucket and I'll bring my shovel."

"See ya, Grandpa!" he said, and slammed down the receiver.

Sunday was a total joy. Samantha felt well and was delighted to be a part of my family. Nicholas loved her and taught her how to put a worm on a hook. She asked me to take her shopping for a gift as soon as I told her she was invited by the birthday boy, and she chose a king-sized bubble wand. Nicholas shrieked with delight as the massive bubbles floated over the lake, refusing to pop. Samantha told me quietly that she could picture herself floating just like those bubbles when her time came - hovering, floating, and hating to leave me. The photos she snapped that day showed more than we expected to see. One showed a bubble within a bubble - twin souls, just like the two of us.

After lunch, Nicholas carried slices of his birthday cake to each of us. He had asked his dad to put strawberry ice cream on Samantha's.

"I knew you would want strawberry, Samantha," he announced proudly, as he carefully handed her the paper plate. "I know Grandma and Grandpa only like chocolate."

"Thanks, Nicholas," she laughed. "You are a remarkable young man. I'm so happy you invited me to celebrate your birthday."

"I knew you wanted to come, so I told Grandpa to call you."

Nicholas moved next to her chair and reached around her shoulder just enough to give her a quick hug, and then he ran off to get more cake for the others. We stayed in the park until twilight. I knew the day with my family helped give her the emotional strength she deserved.

Samantha was scheduled to have a table at the November psychic fair, but I knew it was impossible for her to spend the day doing readings. I convinced her to let me go in her place. The two-day event went smoothly, even though I was extremely nervous taking on her clients. I called her several times to tell her how things were going. She was excited that the fair was bringing in a lot of people, and even more excited that I was sitting at her table. On Sunday evening it was over and I was exhausted. I felt like I could sleep for a week, yet I was anxious to get back to her. I planned to give her the money I earned to cover her mounting medical bills.

She was waiting at the door for me, looking pale and tired, but smiling. I got a huge welcoming hug.

"Oh, thank you William. You did well," she said, clutching at the back of my jacket.

"All for you, Samantha. But I have to tell you this is nothing compared to all you've done for me. Are you feeling OK?"

"Pretty well. I had a little trouble with my breathing today, but I went to the drugstore for an inhaler..."

"Oh, no. I could have picked one up for you. How did you drive in that condition?"

"Well, I sat in the car for a long time trying to catch my breath. I'm sure it was just a panic attack, because I felt better when I calmed down."

"It doesn't sound right to me, Samantha. I think we should go to the hospital."

"*No*, I'm all right. The inhaler worked. I don't want to go back for any more tests."

"Let's talk more tomorrow. I'll tell you all my stories after you've gotten some rest. If you feel bad during the night, I want to know immediately. Even if you call 911, you have to let me know, somehow."

"I promise I'll call you. You know I can't wait to hear every detail of the fair."

I woke up the next morning at 10:00 feeling as though I hadn't slept. Fearing the worst, I quickly dialed her number.

"Samantha, thank goodness you're all right. We had a rough night, didn't we?"

"I could hardly breathe."

"I know."

"William, I feel like I don't have any time left. There's so much more you need to know. When are you coming over?"

"I'll be there in half an hour. I'll bring something from the bakery."

The door was open when I arrived and she was at the kitchen table. Her face was nearly as colorless as the night I rushed her to the hospital. I made two cups of instant coffee and cut the apricot coffee cake. It was another of her favorites. I told her everything I could remember about the fair and how everyone asked about her.

"Samantha, it wasn't the same without you. I don't know what I'll do if you leave me."

"I have to leave. The choice was made a long time

ago."

"But, we're so connected. I think that when you die, I'll die. I think you're going to take me with you."

"I won't take you with me. You are to stay here - right here with Julia. Trust me on that and know it's very important. I'm not sure how it will work, but *there is a way*."

"You're a part of me, Samantha. You said it yourself when you told me we were twin souls. Julia feels it too. She asked me if we were having an affair."

"I thought that would happen."

"I told her no, of course, but I know I'm having an affair in my heart. I feel as if I'll weaken and take my own life when you leave me. I don't know if I'll be strong enough to stay here without you."

"You must be strong, and you will. Please don't do anything like that. I need you here with Julia."

it would be easy to fall in love with you, william...but it's too late.

My nights became restless as I continued to feel Samantha's discomfort. One night in my dreams, I went to a field. I found myself sitting on an old-fashioned quilt...there were flowers all around me. Samantha came and sat with me and told me things, but I couldn't remember any of it when I awoke. I called her the next morning and asked if she had any recollection of a quilt in her dreams.

"No, I don't think so," she said quietly. "But I'm sure that's where we will meet after I cross. It will be our place."

I went to the field many times after that.

I started grocery shopping for Samantha so that she

would have one less thing to worry about. Her list was never very long, but she loved fruit - especially oranges - and I bought the biggest oranges I could find. We would sit and share stories and sandwiches and orange sections.

I put dinners in her freezer, but she never ate them. She preferred the ham sandwiches or chicken salad I picked up at the deli. In truth, the time we spent together was more important to us than any home-cooked meal.

Just after Thanksgiving, I brought Samantha to my house because I wanted her to be with me when I decorated the Christmas tree. I figured if Julia woke up, I'd deal with it. Samantha curled up on the couch and I lit a small cone of incense in a seashell and turned on some holiday music.

"I think I'll lie down right here while you put on the ornaments," she said.

I went to my room and brought my pillow to tuck under her head. That sweet smile of thanks made me want to kiss her once again, but it didn't seem appropriate.

As I worked, I realized she had fallen asleep and she wasn't breathing right. She would stop breathing, and in what seemed like forever, catch her breath again. I thought she was going to die right there in front of me. When I took her back home that night, I wished I could have stayed.

A few days later, my fears became reality. I had to take her back to the hospital because she couldn't catch her breath. I followed her doctor into the hall after he talked with Samantha and made several notes on her chart.

"Doctor, please tell me it was just a panic attack."

"The medication, vitamins and kelation didn't work, William," he said. "She probably only has a month."

I fell back against the wall and it took some time to regain my composure. But then I turned on him in anger.

"How can you say that? You're robbing her of her control and she's not going to buy into that! You aren't giving her any hope!"

When I walked back into Samantha's room, she knew by the look on my face that the doctor had given me the prognosis. She reached for my hand to send whatever strength she could.

"You know, William," she managed, "I look in the mirror and I'm an old woman. I'm finished here. I don't have anything more to do."

The doctor waited patiently, knowing he had said what was necessary so that Samantha could make some final decisions.

"Can I go home?" asked Samantha.

"I'll sign you out in the morning," he assured her. "I don't think I have to ask if you have someone to look in on you, do I?"

I assured him in an instant with, "No, you don't have to ask. I want to be the one she calls."

I was in total despair, but I knew it was important to keep a positive attitude for Samantha. She asked me to be her liaison with the doctor because she brought home medicine that made her feel confused. She said she "couldn't think straight." This woman, who was highly intelligent - read book after book until she had filled two bookshelves the length of a room - could not think straight.

I put her medicine in individual cups marked morning, noon, and night for each day of the week, and I sorted her household bills so we could pay them together. I could tell by her telephone conversation with her daughter that she was content enough with a call, but it hurt me that she was not given enough time or strength to make the trip to Montana as we planned.

Her eyes sparkled the morning I showed up with a tiny Christmas tree, complete with lights and an angel. She said if she ended up in the hospital again, she would unplug it and take it with her. The stocking I stuffed with packages of cashews made her laugh.

"You know, when I was a kid," she said, "I used to pick out a little bag of cashews as a prize for being good at the grocery store. How did you know they were my favorite kind?"

"How do I know anything?" I asked. "How do I take your pain? We're like one person, Samantha."

I was lighting the fireplace when she sat down on the hearth next to me.

"William, promise me again that you won't do anything foolish when I pass. Promise me you will stay in your house with Julia at least until after Christmas."

"What does Christmas have to do with it?"

"It's important, William. Promise me."

"I'll promise you anything," I said, but I didn't understand what she meant.

CHAPTER FIFTEEN

I'm not sure what night the dream came. Samantha and I were standing at a window. I think it was a window in a hospital room. We turned to hug each other and I bent down and kissed her. I heard myself saying, "*Do you know how long I've waited to do this?*" She said, "*When did this all happen?*" And I said, "*I'm not sure.*" Samantha had her bag packed and I was walking her out of the room saying, "*We have the rest of our lives.*" I woke up smiling and then I realized where I was.

I never did tell Samantha about the dream. I figured she would repeat that we could never fall in love. But it was way too late for me. I was deeply in love. One thing she told me I'll never forget. She said I gave her quality of life, if not quantity, and I brought back her music and rainbows.

I guess my birthday on the sixteenth of December would have slipped by had it not been for the thoughtfulness of Rodney's meditation group. They wanted to get together with me for lunch and it would be my choice of restaurants. I knew I wanted to take Samantha if she was up to it, so I suggested we all meet at her favorite, Taste of China off Douglas Avenue.

It was a beautiful, sunny Tuesday. It was a treat to be back with my old friends and a *special* treat since Samantha was able to be there. Mark joined us for lunch too, and he was fascinated with the conversation around the table. He and Samantha were seated next to each other, and I could tell they were totally comfortable with each other. I watched the two of them with delight, and my mind drifted back to the stories and laughter I'd shared with each of them. Samantha caught me lost in my thoughts.

"Mark, look at your dad. He's someplace else! And he's the one driving me around this city."

He laughed along with her. "He's someplace else, all right. But you know, this is the happiest I've ever seen him. It's a special day for me to meet the friends he works with."

We continued to laugh and tell stories, and we finally walked out to the parking lot to say goodbye. Samantha was very tired and I knew I had to get her home. It was on the drive back that she told me she had a surprise birthday gift picked out for me, but she was sorry it didn't get finished on time. I wondered how she could have shopped without my knowledge, but I let that question pass and told her that she was the only gift I needed. I also told her I was happy she felt well enough to go to my party.

"I know I teased you in the restaurant about driving me around in some sort of *spaced-out* mode, but I need one more ride to the hospital tomorrow. There's one other test the doctor wants me to have. I can't imagine what he thinks he can do at this point."

"I'll be there, Samantha. And trust me, I knew you were kidding around about my drifting. But I have to admit, I've been doing it a lot lately."

She handed me a book the next morning when she met me at her door.

"What's this?"

I glanced at the title - *Letters From The Light*.

"All I do is run up and down the highway with you. I'm not going to have time to read this."

"You will," she replied. "Put it by your bed."

And then she shared the best news I could have gotten.

"Sarah called just before you drove up. She and Adam are flying in tonight to see me. When I told her I'd be in the hospital, she said they'd get a rental car at the Des Moines airport and visit me in Ames. Isn't it great news?"

"Oh, it's the best news I ever heard." I laughed along with her and gave her a hug.

"You can just drop me off, and Sarah will bring me home tomorrow."

"It sounds like a good deal, Samantha. You need time with her and Adam and it doesn't matter *where* you are - just so you're together."

The drive to the hospital was far different from our other trips. It was upbeat and reminiscent. I saw a different Samantha. The mind can make or break the body.

I waited out the day, wishing I had not agreed to leave the hospital, yet knowing how important it was for her to have quality time with Sarah and Adam.

On Thursday afternoon, I got a disturbing call.

"William?"

"Samantha! God, I missed you. How was your test? Did Sarah and Adam get there all right?"

"They didn't come," she sobbed.

"*WHAT*?"

"They didn't come," she repeated, sniffing back her tears.

"You mean I left you there a day and a half, taking

God knows what test, and they didn't show up? What in the hell happened?"

"I called her twenty minutes ago and she said she was sorry, she'd have to make it another time. There was no explanation, William. I'm just sick. I don't know what to do..."

"I'm coming to get you right now!"

The drive to Ames during rush hour was unbelievable, and I was furious as well. The only daughter she had, and she offered her mother no explanation. I thanked God for the time Samantha had with my small family and the fact that I could be there for her. She had no one else.

When I found her room, she was dressed and sitting in a chair. She looked pitiful. Her pale face was tear-stained and drawn. The smile that normally greeted me did not come. I took her hand and helped her to her feet and held her in my arms.

"Samantha, it's all right now. I'm here. I'll take care of everything. Let's get out of here."

"Oh, William, how many times have you rescued me? I can't even count."

I stopped at a diner a few blocks from the hospital because Samantha insisted on buying my dinner. We finally shared a laugh when she realized she had no money with her and I would have to spring for the check. She ate some soup and a few bites of her sandwich before she relaxed and began to rationalize the situation.

She knew she had to let go of the hurt and take care of herself. It seemed the test was a waste of time and the doctor was sending her home - possibly for the last time. I couldn't bear it. I assured her over and over that I would never leave her.

Samantha had an inner strength and beauty I recognized from the first day we met and she managed to pull a portion of it to the surface. She wanted to ride along on Friday when I ran errands, and she marveled at the changes Mother Nature had brought us with the first light snowfall. She wanted to stop at both restaurants we had been haunting all year, and we chatted with the waitresses and owners. We had a remarkable day. I hated to see it end, and I knew she had to feel the same way.

Driving back, she found a romantic tune on the radio and began to sing along.

"Samantha, your voice is beautiful!"

"Listen to the refrain, William. The words are so perfect."

She went on singing and then - she stopped.

"Oh, I'm out of breath. I can't sing any more. You can sing to me."

"I can't sing…no way."

"Try it, William."

I started to follow along, and my voice blended with the radio.

impossible.

"You're doing very well," she laughed, and we sang together to the end of the song.

"You shouldn't be surprised at anything anymore, William. We blend perfectly in everything we do."

Then she quieted and said, "Can you stop the car a minute? There's something I want to tell you."

"Sure."

I pulled over on the embankment and turned off the ignition.

"What?" I asked, half smiling.

131

"Here I am, sick, and I'm still happy. I don't get it; I don't even feel like a person any more."

"Well, how do you feel?"

"I feel like a *nothing*."

"You don't look like a *nothing* to me," I said calmly. "You're sitting right here next to me and you are definitely a *something*. You are a person - believe me," I assured her.

"But I can't do things any more. You do everything for me."

"I want to help you, Samantha. I want to do everything for you."

She was quiet.

"William, I have to tell you this before it's too late...I love you."

I was surprised by her boldness, but then I knew it was time to say what was in my heart.

"I know you do, Samantha. I love you too."

She started to cry and I pulled her against me.

Cars were flying past us and horns were honking but we were oblivious to everything. We sat there for a long time and then finally, she looked up at me and we kissed. There was nothing more - just a sweet, tender kiss. I'd been waiting for that moment and it finally came. She snuggled against my chest and I will never forget the love I felt in my heart at that moment. After a while, she sat back and leaned closely against my side as I started the car.

I hated that I couldn't spend Saturday with her, especially after we declared our feelings the night before. Julia was right about my absence on weekends. It was due to Samantha's illness, but I had to start spending more time at home.

I received a call from Dr. Vargas inviting me to his holiday party. I decided it would be interesting to visit with colleagues I hadn't seen for nearly a year, and I wondered what they would think of the *new* William.

Naturally I was on my own. Julia could not, or would not, leave the house with me. The barriers were very real and we respected each other's territory to avoid an all-out war.

I left for the party at eight, but as I started toward the downtown area, I had a strange feeling Samantha needed me. I turned around and headed toward her house. She was delighted to see me, but she was weak and gray-looking compared to the day before. As soon as she saw me, she fell into my arms.

"God, I missed you today, Samantha. Are you all right?"

"I'm really tired," she said, softly. "I guess I'm worn out from yesterday."

She took my hand and we walked into the kitchen. She had several candles burning on the buffet and there was a single place-setting at the round oak table. I picked the high-back chair next to hers and sat down.

"Do you want to split this last big orange with me?" she asked, as she began to tear away the pealing.

"I'll take one section, I guess. I'm not really hungry. I'm on my way to a party with the guys I used to work with at the hospital, but I wanted to stop and make sure you were all right. Besides, I hate not seeing you on weekends. Is that all you're eating for supper?"

"No, I ate something earlier. William, I wish you weren't going to that party tonight."

"If it's Julia you're worried about, you can forget it. She's not going with me."

"It doesn't matter whether or not Julia goes," she defended.

"You're the one I want to take, Samantha."

"You know I'd want to go if I felt better. I'd love to watch the interaction. You haven't forgotten your past. You've only lost the emotional ties with the work. Anyway, you should get going, and you shouldn't worry about me. I'm really tired, William. I'm going to bed early."

I got up and leaned down to put my arms around her.

"I need a stand-up hug," she said, as she rose to face me.

We held each other for a long time.

At 5:30 the next morning, the telephone startled me. It was Samantha and it sounded like she was in a tunnel.

"Are you OK?" I asked.

"No, I don't feel well. I'm having trouble breathing."

"Oh, God! Do you want me to take you to the hospital?"

"I won't go back to that hospital!"

"Well, then I'm coming over."

"No! Listen to me, William. Listen to me very carefully. I need you, but don't come over for a while. Just wait a few hours."

"What? A few hours? All right, whatever you say. Do you want me to stop at the supermarket and pick up some groceries?"

"No, don't do that. I just need some help with my medicine."

I knew something was different about that phone call. She was vague and her voice sounded distant. Did I have to wait a *few hours*? Should I go now? I paced the floor. It was still dark outside. Why would she call so early about sorting medicine? It made no sense. Suddenly my chest tightened. I knew.

i'm not afraid to cross...you have to let me go when the time comes.

I grabbed my car keys and ran for the door. I saw nothing but pavement as I pushed the accelerator to the floorboard.

don't be foolish...i love you dearly...if you do anything foolish, we can never be together...

I turned into her driveway and slammed the transmission into park. I froze in my seat the instant I realized my chest was totally free of pain.

My shoes felt like lead and the steps appeared higher as I climbed them in record time and pounded on the door. There was no answer, no sound. I used my key and went in; there was silence. I walked into the bedroom and hit the ceiling light.

oh, no!

"*SAMANTHA!*" I screamed.

I rushed to her and grabbed her shoulders. I shook her and put my ear to her chest. There was nothing; her sightless eyes stared at me.

"*SAMANTHA! PLEASE WAKE UP!*"

I must have dialed 911, but I don't remember doing it. The police were there and the ambulance screamed outside. Mark came to get me but I don't remember calling him. I don't know how my car got home.

Julia was blocking the door when Mark pulled opened the screen for me. She was staring at me - just staring at me.

"*I HOPE YOU'RE HAPPY NOW! SHE'S DEAD*!" I screamed in her face.

It was December 21st - the Winter Solstice; the day of power. She had passed on the strongest spiritual day of the year.

CHAPTER SIXTEEN

They tell me I was hysterical for weeks, but somehow I managed to call all the readers I could find who were friends of Samantha's. I don't remember doing it. Her daughter was notified and flew into town to make arrangements for cremation and a memorial service. I don't remember calling her. I thought the memorial service was a month after her death. It was only eight days. I'm told I took the microphone at the memorial service, but I don't know what I said.

When I think back to those days, I see myself in the recliner, crying uncontrollably. Mark and Julia are walking around me but I don't hear them talking. I remember Julia taking me to a doctor for Valium. I only remember one thing about that visit: I ended up sitting on the edge of my bed pouring the contents of the Valium bottle into my left hand.

"WILLIAM, THE PHONE IS FOR YOU," called Julia.

I put my glass of water on the nightstand and picked up the receiver.

"Yes?"

"Is this William?"

"Yes."

"My name is Carolyn Reynolds. You don't know me, but I got your number from Rodney. I'm an old friend of Samantha's. Are you still there?"

"...Yes."

"I have a message for you from Samantha."

"*WHAT? TELL ME!*"

"This is what I got:

'i love you dearly, but don't do anything foolish. we cannot complete our work if we are both on the same side. you must stay on the earth plane. i cannot connect with you until you calm down. the tears are good...they will help you heal. remember we are but a veil apart. i will reach you if you allow me. give more time and we will once again be connected.'

"Does that sound right to you?"

"Yes, that sounds right! She's the only one who would use those words!"

"William, I feel a strong love coming from her. It transcends a male/female relationship."

"Yes, I understand that too, because we're twin souls. You must call me again if you get anything else. Will you promise?"

"I'll call you."

The Valium rolled across the nightstand as I turned off the light and got into bed. Within seconds I felt the mattress go down next to me! The tears started and I tried to fight them. I recognized her energy - I knew it was Samantha. I felt her hand on the side of my face, wiping away my tears. Even though I tried to control myself, I sobbed. Her energy left as quickly as it came. My emotions got in our way.

i'm so sorry, samantha! come back to me!

I had a determination to calm myself so we could be together somehow, and the next day I went over and over our conversations in my mind. I picked up the book on my nightstand - the book Samantha gave me before she died - *Letters from the Light*. And it was just that. It was a book of letters that were dictated by the spirit of a dead man. Ms. Elsah Barker wrote his words in 1914 as they came to her, page after page. The real shock came when she told of numbness and redness in her left hand and arm when the spirit reached her. I realized Samantha had been training me for the last four months!

she'll try to reach me from beyond through my hand!

Did I believe it? I wanted to believe it. I relaxed across the bed with my arms at my sides. There was nothing. I relaxed from my forehead to my toes, counted backward from a hundred, held my thumb to my first finger and asked my guides for help. Nothing. I moved my left arm up over my stomach and tried again. Nothing. How long was this going to take?

here i am...do something!

Time was moving slowly for me. The nights were sleepless and the days seemed endless. I tried everything I could think of to get myself under control but the depression was overwhelming. I played her death scene over and over in my mind. When I closed my eyes, I saw dead eyes looking back at me. I had to force myself to eat, and sometimes I couldn't keep the food down.

If only I hadn't gone to the holiday party. She didn't want me to go, but I did. Why didn't I stay with her that night? Maybe there would have been something I could have done for her. Had I stayed, she might still be alive! Why would God give me the love of my life, my twin soul, and then take her away? Telephone calls came, but I let the recorder fill to capacity. I wanted to hear no words, except her words - *i love you.*

Then, in what seemed like overnight, there was a

definitive change in Julia. Mark told me she cancelled a Christmas party she planned for teachers from her school and invited friends and family instead. She told Mark she thought I needed my family for comfort since Samantha passed. I couldn't see it at the time, though. To me, it was an invasion. I went down the hall to my office and closed the door. I couldn't stop the tears. I opened my computer and began to type a journal:

December 24:
today is christmas eve. julia invited a house-full of company. hopefully i will feel better with people around me. i'm glad i put up a tree for you and brought cashews for you in the red stocking. i know now why i did it so early...you were not supposed to have christmas with me.

When the guests left the party, I stumbled back to my desk in tears.

i don't know who was here or what gifts I opened tonight...i just wanted the night to be over...music was something we shared, samantha...you said i brought your music back to you. now music can't help me...it only causes more tears. i wish i could have one more hug. people asked me if i've been sick. i have dark circles under my eyes...i do look sick.

Christmas day was no better.

December 25:
i am so sad. i looked into the mirror and saw dead eyes. it's as if my soul is gone and I am empty.

December 27:
i'm going to get off these pills before i get hooked. i will talk to your daughter tomorrow...i hope she's ok. i need permission to look for information on your computer. i tried to reach you today but failed. i get too excited and i can't get to you.

December 29:
today was your memorial service and it was a blur. the weather was bad and not many people came. the minister handed me the microphone, but that's all i remember. i hope i didn't make a fool of myself, or of you. i feel you saying i looked nice - that i did fine. thank you.

December 30:
i've been alone all day. i can't quit crying. i can't accept the fact that you are gone. i tried to pull you through my solar plexus but i couldn't...it was very painful. i didn't know what i was doing. you have to help me. i got a message through rodney today. he gave me the words, "blue rose." i know the message is from you. he could not have known the words you gave me when we worked together. tomorrow is new year's eve. i'll be glad when this year is over.

I was grateful to have Julia at home with me during her holiday break, and I sensed a change in her. Her temperament through the holidays was surprising and most welcome. She was sympathetic to my needs and wasn't drinking. I saw no signs of withdrawal - no shaking, no sweats. I couldn't understand it. How bizarre it was to think the tables had turned and it was William who was addicted - addicted to grief.

I was still in a desperate state in the new year. Julia understood my pain and decided to take off work a few extra days. She planned a two-day trip to the Ameristar Casino, of all things, on the Missouri River bordering Nebraska. To my dismay, I found the 128 miles of road meant to heal me, were causing immeasurable pain. I was being reminded of my times on the road with Samantha.

And then I found myself in the flashing lights of the Ameristar and got caught up in the tunes of the gaming machines. It was just what I needed. We checked in, got personal cards and headed for the "slots." We did well and then not so well, but I was having fun. Suddenly I felt a twinge in my left hand. I pushed back my chair and rested my forearm on my lap.

what's going on? is it finally you?

"William, what's wrong?" Julia asked. "Did you hit your arm on something?"

"Uh, no!" I laughed. "Watch this!"

My hand started moving slightly and began to turn red.

"Oh, my God, William! What happened? This isn't funny."

"It's *Samantha*!"

I felt like I was going to cry, but I knew I couldn't or she wouldn't be able to hold the energy. I sucked in a deep breath and started to count to ten. I had to stay calm.

"Ask her what machine to play," Julia laughed. "If she's really there, she'll know."

"It's her energy in my hand, that much I know, but I don't know how to ask questions. I've been waiting for this. She said she would be able to reach me if I stayed calm. Let me try something."

"Ok, *Samantha*," I said, choking back my emotion, "tell me when to play two quarters."

I started feeding the cherry machine, one quarter at a time.

"You're nuts," laughed Julia. "That's so ridiculous. It will never work."

After about five or six plays, my hand started to move slightly to one side.

"Julia, watch this," I said, and I put in two quarters. The machine chimed and I won $13.

"Do it again!" she laughed.

I did it again and again. It was unbelievable. Within a short time I'd won back the $40 I lost earlier. I tried asking her other questions to see if I could get a response, but I couldn't.

"William, if you keep talking to your hand, they'll take you away."

"Do you think I care?" I laughed, and kept talking.

Julia was excited about winning, but I didn't care about the money. Samantha finally came to me. I felt myself getting stronger. We had done it! And when I couldn't hold the energy any more, she was gone.

I missed talking to her every day. I missed seeing her. But now I knew she could reach me.

When we got back to Des Moines, I headed for my room and closed the door. I sat on the bed with my left arm on my lap and concentrated on bringing in Samantha. I waited patiently to see if anything would happen. It didn't take long. My hand started to move slightly.

"Show me *yes*," I said.

I waited. My index finger rose slowly and then shot up at an angle.

"Not so hard!"

"Show me *no*." I said.

My little finger started to move and it shot up also.

"Ouch, not so hard!"

I was really excited. We could hook in to each other any time we wanted with this ideomotor response. I needed her as much as she needed me, but there had to be a better signal - one with a little less force!

January 5:

i don't know who turned on my radio in the middle of the night. was it you? the song was the same one you sang in my car the day you told me you loved me. i know you don't want me to lose the music, like you did ...if only it didn't make me cry.

I went to your house today and i stood on the porch for a long time. i saw sarah and she's doing ok. i adore adam. he hugged me, so i'm sure he felt you. children are so in tune. your daughter has the key now, and i have your work here at home.

Ten days later I got a call from a jeweler near my house.

"Is this William?" he asked.

"Yes."

"William, your name was left with me a few months ago as an alternate to pick up an order here. A lady named Samantha came in to buy a gift and told me to call her when it was ready. She told me that she would be in the hospital quite often and that I should call you if she wasn't at home."

"I don't know what you're talking about," I answered.

"Are you the man who came in with Samantha to have her diamond ring repaired?"

"Yes, I am."

"Well, I have something here for you. She said it was your birthday present."

"Thank you so much. I'll be right up." I could feel the tears beginning again.

When I walked into the store, the jeweler was waiting for me.

"You're William, aren't you. I remember. You and Samantha were laughing about being twin souls and you were trying on my rings. Come into the back room with me and sit down a minute."

I was a wreck, but what was new? I followed him beyond a curtain and into his small workroom.

"William, this is yours," he said quietly, and handed me a blue velvet box.

I snapped open the top and found a ring with two birthstones wrapped in silver. I knew the story immediately. When Samantha and I were trying on rings that day, she said it was sad that none of them had our birthstones. My gift was a ring with my stone for December, a turquoise, and her stone for September, a sapphire.

"I'm sorry it took so long to get it to you, William, but Samantha wanted real stones set in - not the synthetic stones I usually carry. And she also requested a diamond on each side. I prepared an appraisal for your insurance. The ring is valued at $300."

I was floored. Samantha didn't have extra money

to spend on a gift for me. I would have been just as thrilled with the $69 synthetic.

"Are you sure this should be mine?" I asked. "She died recently, and maybe the ring should go to her daughter."

"No, the ring is for you. It's your birthday present. And William, I'm so sorry to hear about Samantha. Please accept my sympathy."

I put the ring on my right hand, small finger, and thanked him again. I was still a mess when I got home, but I wanted to show the ring to Julia. I told her it was a twin-soul ring and it was a birthday present from Samantha. She quietly accepted the fact that I wanted to wear it. I was relieved, but didn't understand her reaction. She simply reached out, turned the ring on my finger and said no more. I assumed she no longer felt threatened since her so-called rival was dead.

That same evening, Julia came running into my office.

"William, you have to help me! My sister's house is in the path of a storm coming in off the Atlantic. I just heard it on Channel 13."

"Julia, that's terrible. Do you want to work with me on this?"

"Anything you say," was the answer. And it wasn't the answer I expected to hear.

We walked into the living room, and I turned off the news program.

"Give me both of your hands. Good, now let's close our eyes."

"All right, visualize Andrea's house in Virginia Beach. Now I want you to see a gigantic white light over the top of the roof. Bring down the light and wrap it like a white sheet around and under the entire house. This is going to be the white light of protection."

We were quiet for another few minutes.

"That's it, Julia. You can open your eyes. We'll see what happens."

She smiled and thanked me and left the room as if it was something she did every day. She was changing right in front of my eyes.

The phone rang the next evening after dinner. It was Andrea, so I quickly passed the phone to Julia. I already knew everything was fine, and Julia's conversation verified the fact. She passed the phone to me, smiling and nodding.

"William, I had to talk to you! Our house is the only house on the block that didn't have major damage. We're sitting right in the middle of everything and we're fine. Julia told me what you did and I want to thank you for helping us. You made a believer out of me today."

"You're welcome, Andrea, and I'll send your thanks to Julia too. We worked on this together for the first time. I'm grateful that you and your family are safe."

CHAPTER SEVENTEEN

I went to my room that night still confused about Julia's eagerness to join me in protecting her sister's house. Was she just happy to be a part of anything to help Andrea? I couldn't sleep, so I went to my computer to enter my thoughts and to thank Samantha for the surprise birthday gift.

January 16:
my dear samantha...how do i begin to thank you for the ring...i am overwhelmed with happiness and i will never take off this special gift from you. i hope you are with me like this forever until i can join you again.

I was in such a relaxation; I guess I didn't realize my hands were moving across the keyboard very rapidly. I went to bed feeling totally exhausted, and the next morning when I walked into my office, this is what I found on my screen in capital letters:

YES I AM WITH YOU. I AM GLAD YOU ENJOYED THE RING. THE STONES ENTWINED LIKE WE DID. THE RING REMINDS YOU WE ARE ALWAYS TOGETHER. YOU ARE BECOMING A WISE PERSON. I KNOW YOU WILL MAKE ME PROUD AS I STAND BESIDE YOU. BUT KNOW I AM HERE. I LOVE YOU DEARLY.

I couldn't believe my eyes. Samantha reached me through my hands! I must have typed her words as i drifted. I hadn't intentionally set the capitalization on my computer...at least I didn't remember. I didn't remember anything except feeling very tired and going to bed. Oh, my God! I was literally communicating with Samantha and her words were on my screen! No one would ever believe this.

I hit the "save" icon and decided to leave my computer running 24 hours a day, if that's what it took...just in case she could do it on her own. It was unbelievable that I could have gone that far into spirit and still typed in the words.

I must have walked into my office a dozen or more times that day, hoping something would appear on the blank screen. It was driving me crazy. I wanted to tell someone. All my friends knew I was nearly over the edge with grief. I remembered hearing, "...there's a fine line between genius and insanity."

It was hard to concentrate on anything, so I put on my coat and took a walk in the cold winter air of Des Moines. I must have walked for miles. But if I thought fresh air would work, I was wrong. My mind was spinning out of control. I missed Samantha so much. I knew we would always be together, somehow, because that's what she continually taught me. Was this the avenue she chose? Was there more to come?

I sat at my computer at bedtime and typed, trying to meditate at the same time. How in the world was I able to do it the night before? No matter how I concentrated, I couldn't make contact with Samantha. I went to bed, feeling totally lost and alone. She left me broken and I knew I would never be whole again.

The January psychic fair was coming up in another week, and I was looking forward to seeing my friends again. Julia shocked me by suggesting she would love to

go with me and see what it was all about. What in the
world was going on with her? She came in from school
one day and announced she was going to darken her hair
and maybe go shopping for a curling iron. Said she had a
feeling she wanted a change...and did I think I'd like to see
her dress up a little once in a while?

    hell, yes!

I was catching a cold and wondered whether or not
I should even go to the fair, but I wanted to put a photo of
Samantha on her table and a stack of paper so people
could write notes expressing their feelings. Julia gave me
a binder from her school supplies so I could make a memory book of everything that came in - another surprise.

We arrived early to set up a memorial table, and
one of the readers lit a candle surrounded with flowers to
complete the display. I placed her photo along with a
poem called, *The Seer*, written by a friend in my meditation group. It was tough for me to see only a photo at that
table instead of the person I loved and respected.

Julia and I wandered around the room, and I intro-
duced her to the readers. I stopped at one of the vendor's
booths and picked up a huge twin crystal.

"Julia, look at this! I have to have it," I shrieked,
studying what appeared to be two stones grown into one.

"So, tell me...what's so special about crystal?"
asked Julia. "The box says, *Clear Quartz*."

"Well, it's also known as rock crystal, and it's one
of the most abundant gemstones we have. The name
crystal comes from the Greek word for ice because the
ancients believed rock crystal was eternally frozen."

"Well, didn't you get smart! Why do so many of
the readers wear crystals?

"The mystic lore is that clear quartz crystal can be used to intensify your intention or desire. You hold or touch the stone while you concentrate on what you want to happen. What do you think?"

"I think you want the one you're holding. And you're certainly wishing hard enough, so I'm going to buy it for you."

who is this i'm talking with? not the julia i know.

We left for lunch and stopped for a few groceries. Julia didn't want to return to the fair, so I helped put everything away and returned on my own. I wanted to be there because I felt very close to Samantha in that atmosphere. I went directly to her table and found that her friends had written lengthy notes. Most of the entries were from fellow psychics, but some were from her old clients who were surprised to find she had passed away.

"Samantha was a person who felt everyone was equal...was very fair to all...always a friend when you needed one...could make you laugh...could cry with you. She taught us well...her legacy will live on...she gave me guidance and direction...a dear friend. Thank you for your insight...thank you for the gift of spirituality. Peace and joy be with you on this your most wonderful journey."

I broke down when I read the things I knew were true about my friend, Samantha, and I was glad I didn't have to try to make excuses for my behavior. Everyone knew how special she was to me, and they were sad to see we were partners on this life path for only a short time. I had an aura picture taken which showed the aura colors of energy surrounding my body, and I could sense from the photo that Samantha was with me. I was surrounded by purple - the wings were a nice touch! It was a good fair.

January 24:
i put a nice picture of you on your table today, but of course you know that. the picture made me cry, but i tried to stay strong for you. the fair was great and everyone did well. it was very crowded. the aura picture was beautiful, and i have no doubt that you are in it with me - your arms surrounding me in purple light. i'm still sick with this cold and i am going to bed.

A few days later, I decided to try to get back to my work as Samantha would have wanted me to do. Step number one was difficult - I took a few messages off the answering machine. A newlywed couple wanted me to come to their home because they felt uncomfortable and wanted it cleared of anything I could find that might cause them harm. I felt Samantha right with me as I cleared the house of dark entities. I knew she was enjoying herself. It was wonderful, although after feeling her presence, I missed her more. It was tough getting to sleep. Julia and I were getting along better, but there had to be an answer for me.

February 12:
i am at my typewriter because i woke up and i can't go back to sleep. you were with me today. i miss you so much. sometimes i feel like i'm breaking apart. thank you for helping me with julia. it has been wonderful having her spend time with me. i know why you insisted we could not be together. i had to stay with julia and continue our work.
I ALSO ENJOYED OUR CONNECTION
i wish i could spend every night with you.
THAT WOULD NOT BE GOOD FOR EITHER

*OF US. WE WILL HAVE NIGHTS TOGETHER. I
HAVE FOUND A NICE PLACE TO TAKE YOU AS
YOU SLEEP. YOU ARE VERY VALUABLE. I WILL
KEEP YOU PROTECTED. DO NOT BE AFRAID.*

February 18:
*i was working with evil again today and i am still
spooked. i can't believe my mind can be taken like that.
i hope you can tell me something about what happened.*
*DEAR ONE YOU ARE SOMETIMES NAÏVE.
GO WHERE I SEND YOU AND THERE WILL BE
ANSWERS. I CANNOT PROTECT YOU FROM
YOURSELF. I AM SORRY I DIDN'T TELL YOU
MORE BEFORE I LEFT. I TRIED. THERE WAS
NOT ENOUGH TIME. I WILL HELP YOU IN YOUR
NEXT LIFETIME.*
*there won't be a next lifetime for me. i'm not
coming back here.*
*WE WILL SEE. I AM VERY BUSY UP HERE
AND WITH YOU. DO NOT THINK YOU CAN EVER
STOP OUR CONNECTION. THE PERSON I KNOW
AND LOVE MUST BE WITH ME. BE MORE CARE-
FUL DRIVING. YOU CANNOT LEAVE NOW. WE
HAVE MUCH TO DO. I CHOSE TO BE THE ONE TO
ASCEND. ONE OF US NEEDED TO BE HERE. YOU
ARE ATTACHED TO YOUR FAMILY AND FRIENDS
AND I HAD NO ONE BUT YOU. I WILL ALWAYS
FIND A WAY TO REACH YOU THROUGH THE
GREAT NETWORK YOU HAVE. REMEMBER I
MADE A PROMISE TO YOU. I WILL NEVER LEAVE
YOU. NOTHING YOU DO WILL EVER MAKE THAT
HAPPEN. REMEMBER OUR LOVE AND HOLD IT*

DEAR. I LOVE YOU DEARLY.

February 23:
help me. i'm so confused about what i am supposed to do here.
I'M TRYING TO HELP YOU. I MISS YOU TOO. I KNOW NOW WE WILL BE TOGETHER. YOU MUST STAY ON THAT SIDE. YOU MUST WAIT. I KNOW I WAS PULLING YOU BEFORE I CROSSED. I TRIED NOT TO. I KNEW YOU SHOULD STAY WITH JULIA AND YOU HAD TO BE THERE BUT I WANTED YOU WITH ME. I KNOW IT WAS HARD ON YOU. I SEE YOUR TEARS AND I WANT TO HELP. WHEN YOU CROSS YOU ARE NOT SUDDENLY ALL-KNOWING. NICHOLAS AND I ARE BECOMING GREAT FRIENDS.
are you playing with nicholas?
I WANT TO KEEP A STRONG CONNECTION WITH HIM. I CAN GET TO YOU THROUGH HIM. HE KEEPS HIMSELF CONNECTED TO YOU.
please make sure this doesn't hurt him.
I WILL KEEP HIM SAFE AND YOU. REMEMBER YOU CAN NEVER DENY MY PRESENCE. YOU FEEL ME WITH YOU.
i miss you. i miss your touch and your hug.
YES AND I MISS YOU. BUT WE ARE LUCKY WE CAN CONNECT. TELL MARK NOT TO GET TOO UPSET. THERE IS A WAY AROUND HIS DELAY.

Messages from Samantha taught me to be more observant of the events surrounding me. Mark, Kate and Nicholas came by unexpectedly on Saturday and I decided to watch Nicholas to see whether or not he got any sense of Samantha in the room. On this day, he simply came in, gave me a hug, and walked across the room to turn on the TV.

Julia was happy to see the kids and Nicholas. I knew Samantha had done something to make her stop drinking. She was changing in other ways as the days progressed. Kate complimented her on her reddish-brown, softly curled hair, that by now, nearly touched her shoulders. She was quite lovely in the black stretch pants, pale blue mohair sweater, and narrow heeled suede boots she bought with her holiday money. I liked the new Julia.

Around noon, Mark and I decided to brew a pot of chili. We took turns adding our favorite ingredients, including a splash of Mark's beer, and we laughed at what we thought the girls and Nicholas would say about our concoction. As we leaned on the counter, the conversation rolled from one thing to another. I walked back to the stove with the intention of giving the chili one more healthy stir before serving time, when I hit something in mid air and felt myself bounce back!

"What's wrong Dad?" asked Mark, as he moved to grab me.

"I think its Samantha!" I laughed.

Mark backed off. He just stared at me.

"No, really, Mark. I feel her energy all through me! She's standing right here!"

At that instant - exactly that instant - Nicholas came running around the corner.

"Grandpa, do you care if I play my piano now?"

samantha, you're here!

"Hey, what a great idea, Nicholas. I'll help you set it up and you can play us a tune while your dad dishes out the chili."

I shot Mark a wink but, from the look on his face, I knew he was puzzled.

i guess it's about time to let mark know what's going on.

I continued my work with renewed energy after having felt Samantha's body against mine. We made another kind of connection. How in the world could that be? Samantha was in the spiritual plane and I was on the earth plane. I really didn't care how she did it; I only wanted her to do it again.

On Monday morning a woman called and said she was very upset because her granddaughter died in an automobile accident and she never had a chance to say goodbye. When she arrived she looked nearly as bad as I looked when Samantha died. Her eyes were hollow - dead like mine. She described what I felt a month earlier.

"William, when I look in the mirror, I don't see anything. There's nothing left of me. My granddaughter was only seventeen. She shouldn't have died at seventeen. God should have taken me! If you can reach her, I'd be forever grateful. I know her death was painful, and I want to know whether or not she's all right."

"Sit with me, Mrs. Carmody, and let me take your hands."

I led her to my office, offered her the large, tan overstuffed armchair I'd chosen for my clients and rolled my computer chair directly in front of her.

I took her hands in mine, but it was really unnecessary. I could already see her granddaughter. I didn't want to just *blurt it out* and frighten her, so the "hands-thing" was a way of making her comfortable and giving her a connection with me. It was, in truth, what she expected.

"Just close your eyes now and relax. What is your granddaughter's name?" I asked.

"Elizabeth Anne Carmody," she replied, calmly.

"Well, I see a beautiful young girl with long blonde hair and blue eyes. She is sitting in a field of flowers in the sunshine...and oh, this is really nice...there are animals all around her. There are hundreds of animals... every kind you can imagine."

"It must be Elizabeth! Tears began to well in the corners of her eyes.

"It *is* Elizabeth."

"But William, you couldn't have known."

"Known what?"

"She was planning to study pre-med and go on to be a veterinarian because she had such a love for animals. I understand what you see. Thank you so much."

"She is telling me there was no pain. It was very fast. She says to tell you she loves you...she says she is happy...she says that all her dreams are fulfilled and she watches for you."

I always felt uplifted when I could bring a spirit to its loved one. I remember so many incidences of a distraught relative finding comfort in knowing his family member or friend was in a good place.

I know there is no bad place when we cross, only a period of healing that all of us must enter until we are ready to return for the good of mankind. We may have been liars, cheaters, self-serving, disrespectful, or criminal, but we must return to life many times until we right our mistakes. When the lessons are learned, we no longer have a reason to return. We remain in spirit life and we are sent to help others as guides or angels. *There should be no fear of death.*

Another experience comes to mind - an eighteen year-old girl who came to ask if I could help her speak to her boyfriend. She was distraught, thinking she had upset him to the point of suicide. She was unable to cope with the depression and pain. She wanted to tell him she was sorry; she felt responsible for his death and needed his forgiveness.

"His name was Carl. I went to school with him...I loved him and then I killed him! I know I killed him!" she sobbed.

I gave her the words as he sent them to me:

"...the first thing I want to tell you is that you were not responsible for my death. I was sent at a time in your life to teach you something...that you could be loved. It was time to move on. I did not commit suicide. I fell asleep and hit the bridge abutment. I loved you and you were the last thing I thought of before I died. You will feel me near you once again. I am here to help."

My life was filled with work once again - the work I was meant to do. Every day was amazing. It was a gift to help others rebuild their shattered lives. But what about my life? I remember telling Rodney one day to heal himself, if he was so powerful. Now I was in his shoes, unable to heal *myself.* My heart was full of pain and I had no answers.

February 26:
julia and i had our anniversary and it's over. neither of us remembered the date and we did the best we could under the circumstances. we are not the same as

we were. i missed being connected with you that day, but i know why you left.

I COULD NOT STAY WITH YOU FOR YOUR ANNIVERSARY. YOU NEEDED TO BE ABLE TO FOCUS YOUR ENERGY IN A DIFFERENT WAY. REMEMBER YOU ARE STILL ON THE EARTH PLANE AND MUST FUNCTION AS SUCH.

When I read Samantha's words on my computer screen, it reinforced the fact that I was stuck on Earth and Samantha was gone forever. I realized that neither my wedding ring nor my twin soul ring could bring back my loves. My wife felt nothing for me; my Samantha was taken from me. I got tears in my eyes remembering the time our waitress saw my wedding ring and said something about how lucky we were to have each other. I smiled at her and didn't know what to say.

"Samantha," I laughed when the waitress moved on, "she thinks you're my wife!"

"Oh, well!" was her answer. I felt the same.

My mind then took me back to a Sunday morning at the hospital when the Chaplain stopped by Samantha's room. We chatted comfortably for about fifteen minutes, and then the Chaplain asked if he could pray with her and her husband.

Samantha looked at him and smiled.

"Oh, he's not my husband. He's married to someone else - he has a family of his own."

The chaplain didn't blink an eye. He just looked at us both and said, "Well, I'd never guess the two of you weren't husband and wife. You look like you belong together." And he took our hands and we prayed together.

A few hours later, the chaplain stepped into the

elevator as I was going down for a sandwich.

"I apologize if I was out of line this morning," he said, and reached to take my hand.

"Oh, no. People make that mistake all the time. We're very close and I guess it shows."

"I saw the look in her eyes and I know you are together in your hearts. Sometimes we are together because God wants it that way. You may not be married on paper, but you are married in your souls."

...married in our souls. i miss you so, samantha. god, i want you back!

I felt like my scull was splitting open. The pain was coming up the back of my neck and crashing in on me.

February 27:

i want you to come and take away my sorrow...when you were here I could call you and you would help me. why did we have so little time?

I AM TRYING TO HELP YOU BUT WHEN I GET YOUR ATTENTION YOU WAKE UP AND THEN WE CANNOT WORK. I AM NOT WILLING TO LEAVE YOU BROKEN. YOU MEAN SO MUCH TO ME. I WANT TO SEE YOU WHOLE. I WANT YOU TO LOOK IN THE MIRROR AND SEE THE WON-DERFUL PERSON EVERYONE ELSE SEES. I AM WORKING ON STORIES FROM HERE AND WE NEED TO START THEM.

stories? what stories?

YOU WILL SEE. THEY WILL BE PUB-LISHED.

can we start now?

NO. MAYBE SOON. WE WILL SEE. WE NEED MORE QUIET TIME. HAPPY ANNIVERSARY. I WANT YOU TO FIND EACH OTHER AGAIN. IT'S IMPORTANT. REMEMBER, I LOVE YOU DEARLY.

February 29:
julia and I went on the gambling boat again as you most certainly know. we had a blast, didn't we? i could feel your excitement. it was just like being with you all day. i loved it…thank you. julia had fun too. she ate egg fu yung at the buffet, but she hates chinese food. i guess she is trying more new things. i feel better today after spending so much time with both of you.
I ALSO ENJOYED THE BOAT. I LIKED SHARING TURNS. I FELT SO CLOSE TO YOU. I WISH YOU COULD FEEL ME, TOUCH ME, SEE ME, AND HEAR ME LIKE I CAN YOU. SOON THAT WILL CHANGE AND THE CONNECTION WILL BECOME EVEN STRONGER. I HAVE PLACES TO TAKE YOU WHEN IT IS SAFE. OUT OF SIGHT IS NOT OUT OF MIND. I HAVE SENT EXTRA PRO- TECTION FOR YOU. SOMEONE YOU TRUST IS NO LONGER WALKING IN THE LIGHT. BE CAREFUL.
samantha, i must ask you this. i want to know that you are not caught on this side. you have crossed over, haven't you?
OF COURSE I HAVE. THIS IS WHAT I CHOSE AND THIS IS WHY I CROSSED. WE COULD NOT FINISH OUR JOBS IF THERE WAS NO CLOSE- NESS. I KNOW YOU MISS ME. I SEE THE TEARS. IT WILL GET BETTER. YOU WILL ONCE AGAIN FEEL MY HUGS. I STILL HAVE MUCH WORK TO

DO ON THIS PLANE. MANY ARE TRYING TO HELP. REMEMBER, I LOVE YOU DEARLY.

please tell me who is not safe for me. who is not walking in the light?

NO. YOU WOULD RUN TO HIS AID, FORGETTING ABOUT YOURSELF. THIS YOU MUST BELIEVE. YOU HAVE A VERY IMPORTANT JOB AHEAD OF YOU. YOU MUST NOT LET ANYONE OR ANYTHING DETER YOU FROM IT. IT IS OF WORLD IMPORTANCE.

CHAPTER EIGHTEEN

I woke up on the morning of March 3rd and went to the kitchen for coffee. Julia was packing her lunch "in between cigarettes." I wished she would have stopped smoking right along with giving up the alcohol, but I decided it was a selfish wish.

"William, why are you up so early? Do you have someone coming over?"

"No."

"You know what? If I were you and I didn't have to leave the building, I'd sleep till noon."

"I'm just a mess, Julia. I can hardly sleep at all any more. Do you want me to finish packing your lunch?"

"OK. Just put in anything you want. I've been eating like a pig lately...actually gained a few pounds. I think I look better, don't you?"

"You really do."

"Are you working on me or something, William? I mean...I feel so much better these days. Even the people at work have noticed a difference."

"I have all my friends working on you," I lied.

I had no idea what was going on. I was just happy for her. I sat at the table with my coffee and watched in amazement as she moved about, gathering papers she had apparently graded the night before. She was wearing black, wool pleated slacks and a matching blazer over a crisp, white linen shirt - so much more chic than the floral ankle length skirts from the year before. She came over, kissed my cheek and was out the door before I could respond.

I watched her back out of the drive, still marveling at the kiss.

The phone rang as I got to my office door, but I let the recorder take it and opened the computer. *OPENED THE COMPUTER?* I never shut it down at night! I hadn't shut it down since I started writing with Samantha for fear I would miss something important. The screen brightened and filled with a message all in caps:

NOW YOU BELIEVE FINALLY. YES I WAS HERE. NOW THINGS WILL PROGRESS FAST. DON'T DOUBT. NOW YOU KNOW IN YOUR HEART. WE ARE NOT HAMPERED BY PHYSICAL. THE MIND WANTS IT AND IT IS. I WILL COME TO YOU. WHEN THE TIME IS RIGHT YOU WILL BE FREE TO TRAVEL WITH ME. YOU WILL LEAVE YOUR BODY AND COME WITH ME. YOU WILL LEARN MANY THINGS.

I fell into the chair and sobbed. It was all too much for me! I called Greg at Iowa State University in Ames...Greg, who had gotten me into this in the first place.

"Greg? Hi, it's William. Can you meet me some-where? I don't know what's going on down here. Samantha is so strong. She tells me she's crossed, but we have this connection."

"Well, a connection is normal for twin souls. I don't consider it a bad thing."

"But, get this - she typed on my computer last night. I opened the screen and I swear it was nothing I wrote. I couldn't begin to author those words!"

"You have to be kidding me! Can I come over now?"

"Oh, man…thanks. I'm about out of my mind. She's been talking with me since right after she died, but never like this. You're the only one I feel I can call."

Greg showed up forty minutes later. I'd saved everything in my hard drive since my first entry on Christmas Eve. It was my way of holding on to Samantha.

"William, this is amazing! Aren't you thrilled to have all these words? I've never seen anything like it; your connection with Samantha is uncanny!"

"I know, Greg, but what does this last part mean? Am I going to die and go with her? I can't! She told me I had to stay here with Julia, and yet, she is coming for me."

"It must mean *astro travel*," he said excitedly. "She will take you in your sleep and return you after you've learned whatever you are to learn. There's nothing to fear."

When Greg left, I felt more comfortable, but I had questions only one person could answer.

is it safe to leave my body now?

NO. NOT UNTIL I TELL YOU. AND I TELL YOU NOT TO COME TO ME. I WILL COME FOR YOU.

did you keep me awake last night?

YOU ARE BEING KEPT AWAKE FOR YOUR OWN SAFETY. DARK WILL ALWAYS TRY TO STOP LIGHT.

how do i leave my body?

PATIENCE IS NOT ONE OF YOUR VIRTUES. I WILL PREPARE YOU FOR THIS.

how and when will you prepare me?

WHEN THE TIME IS RIGHT YOU WILL BE GIVEN PROTECTION. YOU WILL BE FREE.

is there a specific roll greg is to play in this?

YES. HE WILL BE A PROTECTOR FOR YOU. HE WILL PACE YOU AND TALK YOU THRU WHEN YOU ARE UNSURE. WE WILL TAKE A TRIP WHEN YOU CAN TRAVEL. IT IS NOT PHYSICAL TRAVEL.

i miss you.

YES I MISS YOU ALSO. JUST BECAUSE WE CROSS OVER DOES NOT MEAN WE HAVE NO FEELINGS. YOU ARE NOT THE ONLY ONE HURTING. WHEN YOU CROSS YOU SEE THINGS SO MUCH MORE CLEARLY AND YOU SEE THE MISTAKES YOU MADE. SOMETIMES I FEEL THE PAIN I CAUSED YOU BY NOT BEING HONEST AT A SOUL LEVEL. I LOOK BACK AND YOU WERE ONE OF THE MOST IMPORTANT THINGS IN MY LIFE. THANK YOU FOR THE EXPERIENCE OF YOUR LOVE AND LITE. DON'T BE AFRAID. I WILL WALK BY YOUR SIDE.

a friend has asked about elizabeth anne carmody. have you seen her?

YES BUT WE BOTH HAVE OUR WORK HERE AND SPEAK BUT A GLIMPSE. SHE IS ALSO HELPING ONE LEFT ON EARTH. WE WILL HELP BRING MANY TO NEW LITE.

When I finally got to listen to my phone recordings, there was one from a psychic who had a message for me:

"We are together in spirit now and we will be together in life once again. Remember, I love you dearly."

I called and thanked a person I had never met, and assured her I knew the message was for me. Her name was Glenda. The call came from Hannibal, Missouri.

In the late afternoon I made a quick run to the card shop. Samantha's daughter was celebrating her 28th birthday and I thought she would like to know I was thinking about her. I truly wished I could tell her that her mother was still with me. The card shop turned out to be something else. Samantha connected with my hand as I was looking through the birthday selection. The card had to be from me, but Samantha wanted the card to be from her. It was pretty funny, really, and I'm glad nobody saw me fighting with my own hand!

no, i'm not getting that one!

Sarah would have been horrified to get a card that said, *Happy Birthday Dear Daughter.*

What a day. I went to bed with the hope that Samantha would allow me to sleep. I decided to tell her I needed a break. My earth life was supposed to consist of day hours for activity and night hours for sleep. It wasn't my fault that the spirit world knew nothing of time. It must have worked, for one night at least. I woke up the next day knowing I had succeeded in getting the message to her. I was refreshed and ready to work.

In April, another psychic fair was scheduled in the area, and I felt comfortable being there. Julia dropped me off and went to go shopping for summer clothes and a swim suit. She said she wanted to show off at the pool when it opened. Every day was a surprise when it came to Julia. As I got out of the car, she assured me she would be back long before the fair ended, just in case she decided to get a reading. I couldn't believe that one, either.

It was relatively quiet at the fair. Maybe because Spring was in the air and people were enjoying the refreshing change in Iowa's weather. There were no memorials set up this time, but several of Samantha's clients approached me who had not yet heard of her passing. I did very well with their expressions of sympathy, and I wanted to tell them she wasn't really that far away. Of course, I couldn't do that.

Her friends decided it would be nice to plant a tree in her memory at the park, and they began to make plans to get permission from the City Parks and Recreation Department. I agreed, with the assurance that the tree be planted next to the bench Samantha and I adopted, lakeside. It took me a few minutes to recover my composure.

I saw a new face at one of the tables and decided to welcome her.

"Hi, my name is William. Welcome to the fair."

"Oh, thanks," she replied.

She extended her hand to greet me.

"My name is Denise and I know who you are. I met Samantha about a year ago and she told me how much she admired you. Sit down and let me throw out some cards for you."

"All right."

I took the chair in front of her. She was about twenty-five, fair skinned, and had stringy blonde hair. She wore jeans and a western shirt and had a baby sleeping in a car seat just to her left - another example of someone you would never expect to have the gift. She asked me to choose ten cards. I did. A strange look came over her slender face.

"William, forgive me for this, but I see someone

entering your wife."

I felt the blood run out of my head.

"What did you say?"

"Someone is coming into your wife. I don't know how to explain it, William."

I got up immediately. I felt sick. I remember walking away, and that's about *all* I remember.

Richard Novosak, the Geomancy man from St. Louis, stopped me.

"William, ask me a question so I can show you how Geomancy works."

I'm surprised his statement even registered with me.

"Come on, just give me a question!" he badgered. I was shaking and I could feel the sweat around my collar.

"All right," I managed, "how about this…is my wife being taken over by a spirit?"

"I can work with that," he assured me.

I followed him to his table. He wrote my question on the top edge of a form covered with shapes that looked like houses. Then he and handed me four dice about 5 inches long with dots on all sides, not like any I'd ever seen in a board game.

"What are these for?" I asked, nervously. I was a wreck.

"They help to create the pattern I need for Geomancy. Your energy is in the dice, and it creates the pattern of figures I'll use to answer your question. Think about your question, and let the dice roll off your hands when you're ready."

I barely heard him. As I held the dice, a flood of memories came back, but now I was remembering *both* women.

The dice fell on the black African mud cloth. Richard quickly wrote what he read from the dots. I had to throw the dice four more times while he took notes.

just give me my answer, richard!

"What do you see?" I asked with as much patience as I could muster.

"I'll work on this and give you a call at home. What's your phone number?"

"What? Do you mean you can't tell me anything *NOW*?"

"No, Geomancy takes time - hours in fact. If you just want a reading, I can do that."

"I don't want another reading; I want to know what the Geomancy tells you. Here's my number. Call me as soon as you get something."

I don't remember what I did until Julia showed up at the fair. As soon as I saw her enter the room, I made up a story about not feeling well so she'd take me home. I hit the front door and made a dash for my computer. It took me some time to calm myself before I could start typing.

something's going on. i got a reading at the fair today. help me understand. are you possessing julia?

THE WALK-IN SUBJECT. I DON'T KNOW HOW TO GET THIS TO YOU EXCEPT IT IS NOW TIME FOR YOU TO KNOW. I KNOW YOU CAN SEE THE DIFFERENCE IN JULIA. PLEASE JUST BEAR WITH ME. EVERYTHING WILL BE AS PLANNED. JULIA AND I ARE DOING NOTHING WRONG. THINK OF IT AS SHARING.

this is possession, samantha!

NO. NO IT IS NOT. I DO NOTHING WITH-

OUT PERMISSION. WE ARE SHARING YOU.
no. this is not right. what are you doing?
THIS IS TOO HARD TO EXPLAIN. THIS IS
NOT A BAD THING. I AM A WALK-IN LIKE YOU.
YOU WALKED IN TO BE WITH ME AND NOW I
WALK IN TO BE WITH YOU. IT WILL BE A FEW
MONTHS BEFORE THIS IS COMPLETE. JULIA IS
BEING PULLED TO THE OTHER SIDE. WE HAVE
IMPORTANT WORK TO FINISH.
    you told me you had to be on that side and I had
to stay here. you never said anything to me about walk-
in.
    THIS IS SO HARD TO EXPLAIN. JUST OPEN
UP AND GO WITH IT. THIS WOULD BE EASIER IF
YOU WERE NOT SO AWARE. LOOK HOW SMOOTH-
LY YOURS WENT.
    i thought it was the flu! nothing was right...my
work, my clothes, my food. even now i don't know who i
am.
    YOU ARE MY TWIN SOUL. WE INCARNAT-
ED ON THE SAME DAY MANY LIFETIMES AGO.
YOU PASSED ON AND WE COULD NOT CONNECT.
YOU CAME BACK SO WE COULD HAVE PHYSICAL
TIME TOGETHER.
    we can be together, but julia can't be here...is
that right?
    SHE NO LONGER WANTED TO BE HERE.
SHE CHOSE TO LEAVE. DON'T CRY. IT WILL BE
ALL RIGHT.
    now I'm losing julia also.
    NO YOU ARE NOT LOSING ANYONE. YOU
WILL SEE OUR TWO PERSONALITIES MERGE. I

WISH YOU HADN'T FIGURED OUT WHAT WAS GOING ON. WE WOULD HAVE SWITCHED AND YOU WOULD HAVE NEVER KNOWN. REMEMBER I LOVE YOU DEARLY AND WILL NEVER DO ANYTHING BUT FOR OUR HIGHEST GOOD AND FOR ANYONE CONNECTED TO US.

My hands stopped. It took time for me to snap out of it and read the words. Good God! What did it mean? I never heard of a walk-in...Samantha said she's a walk-in *LIKE ME*! Just who in the heck am I if I'm not William? Is this why Julia is changing?

My head was killing me. I tried to relax and make some sense of it. Someone had to have answers for me. I pulled up the Internet to do a search.

I typed, ...*Walk-in*.

Sure enough. There were paragraphs from people experiencing what I had gone through and descriptions similar to what I saw in Julia! It was unbelievable. I printed off all the pages. At least I could go to sleep knowing I was not alone.

Early the next morning, Julia pushed open my door.

"William, the phone is for you."

"Thanks."

"Yes?"

"William? This is Richard Novosak...with the Geomancy reading."

"Richard, I'm so glad you called. What did you find?"

"I stayed up half the night doing this reading for you. You looked so distraught yesterday. It seems there are two women here. Are you having an affair?"

"*No*, Richard!"

"Well, then we may be dealing with another entity. I think you have a walk-in situation involving your wife and another female. Do you want to know who I think it is?"

"Yes, of course I do!" I answered.

"I think it's Samantha. Does that make any sense at all?"

"Yes."

"It *does*?"

"Richard, I can't believe you found this. Is there anything else you can tell me?"

"I found chaos, separation and confusion from your wife. She is changing...as in a rebirth. I see a dependency problem. Could it be alcohol?"

"Yes."

"I see this has changed. She is rejecting this self-defeating behavior. She has clarity and an improved attitude. I find you first communicating with the entity in mid-January of this year. Does that make sense?"

"Yes."

"Did she appear in your dreams?"

"More than that, Richard."

"OK. I found your wife has a curiosity in developing spiritually. It surfaced toward the end of January. Is that true?"

"Yes."

"*Walk-in* is showing up all over the board, William. It looks as if there will be many changes and a completion by the end of the year."

"I've already seen changes. Can I help her?"

"No. As far as you're concerned, you should

regard her as an equal partner in your marriage and you should not impose unrealistic abilities on her. She will have to deal with any unfinished work left by your wife as well, and it will take some time. There are many differences in personalities here. One similarity is this - the entity as well as your wife had trouble relating to family."

"Yes."

"I did some figures on you also, William, and I see you resisting the walk-in phenomenon."

"I just can't understand this, Richard. I never heard of a walk-in, and yet I opened the Internet and found other people going through the same thing. Have you seen the site? It's *WE* and it stands for *Walk-ins for Evolution*."

"I've seen the site, but your situation here *is not the same thing*. Those people *don't know who* is walking into them. They only know they've changed - become more spiritual. In this case, we *know* the walk-in. We know the person *IS SAMANTHA*. This is something all together different. It never happens this way!"

"I want Samantha back, but I'm not willing to lose Julia in the process."

"You won't. Her soul agreed to move out and allow this. Permission had to be given. Samantha will *be* Julia. She will remember Julia's past, but not her own. She'll be confused as to how she can do different things…and why she *wants* to do different things. There will eventually be an integration of personalities, but she will not be the person you knew as Samantha."

"How much can I tell her?"

"Tell her nothing."

I thanked Richard for his work, and he promised to send some literature on Geomancy, or what he termed,

174

Terrestrial Astrology.

He told me it was an ancient art that existed in written records 1200 years ago, beginning in North Africa with the marking of dots or lines in the casting of sand. Richard had compared the spiritual house of Julia with the spiritual house of the entity. The mesh at some point validated that Samantha was walking in.

I got back into the web site and wrote notes to a few of the people who had their stories in print. I told them what had been going on to see what kind of answers they would give. None of the people could relate to Julia's experience because they didn't know the identity of who walked into them. The conclusion from the people I contacted was:

"Your wife is being possessed."

Around eleven, I went to the bookstore and said the word "walk-in" quietly to the clerk.

"Sure, we have that," he said brightly, and he led me to a book by Ruth Montgomery, *Strangers Among Us*. I paid for it and went for coffee nearby, opting for a booth in the back. I read slowly and highlighted everything that applied to us. The book convinced me beyond a doubt that it was true. Still, no reference was made to the fact that anyone in her book knew the identity of the walk-in. A common thread linked each experience, however: each walk-in experienced enlightenment and spiritual growth to benefit mankind.

why should i finish reading this book? i'm watching it in person!

I went home with a cautious, but optimistic outlook. I had no idea what was in store for Julia and me. I missed Samantha so much. Was it too much to hope for to feel her presence in Julia? Would it indeed be completed by the end of the year? I wanted to believe it more than anything in the world.

Julia was going from one extreme to the other, emotionally. One minute she was content; the next minute, she was depressed and cold. Was Samantha having difficulty getting through, or was Julia just a mortal with emotional upheaval? I had doubts as to my own sanity.

Julia came in from school at around 4:00 p.m. and found me at the kitchen table reading a few more references in the Montgomery book.

"Hey, what are you reading?"

"Oh, it's just a paperback I picked up today. How was your day?"

"It was OK, I guess. I got turned around at school and the kids were teasing me. They thought it was great fun."

"Turned around?"

"You know - just the usual."

"Just the usual?"

"I don't know. I went the wrong way or something and ended up in the boys' bathroom…pretty embarrassing. I don't know what I was thinking."

"Oh, don't worry about it. It happens to everybody, now and then. Guess your mind was on something else."

"I guess so. How are you feeling today?"

"Me? I'm feeling fine…why?"

"Well, you had me take you home early yesterday from the psychic fair."

"Oh, that! It was a headache. I'm fine today."

"That's good. I was thinking about getting a reading yesterday, remember? Well, I was thinking on the way home that maybe you could do it."

"Not a good idea, Julia. It would be better to have someone else do it for you. At the next fair or something - in a few months. Do you want to go get a sandwich and maybe see a movie?"

"That sounds like a good idea. I think I'd like to get Chinese, OK? I never used to go anywhere. I feel like a different person. I know what you're going to say…it's because I don't drink any more. Why do you think I didn't get sick? You know, like the withdrawal everyone talks about."

"I had my healers working on you."

"That's nice…I'll go change into some jeans so we can get going."

Oh, this was going to be a good trick if I could pull it off. I'd have to be on guard every minute. What was I saying? I *would* pull it off. She'd be devastated if she knew her rival was going to move *in* on her - literally!

Dinner turned out to be a problem and we had to skip the movie. About half way through the meal she told me she wanted to go home…hated Chinese, and why did I bring her to such a place? My God, this was unbelievable. She went to her room and slammed the door. I was unable to help her.

samantha you were here tonight and then you left. i don't understand this walk-in thing. i'm trying, but it doesn't seem right.

THIS WAS ALL PLANNED BEFORE WE INCARNATED. EVERYTHING IS AS IT SHOULD BE. I DON'T KNOW HOW TO HELP YOU WITH THIS. WHEN I ENTER AND SPEND TIME IN

JULIAS BODY I CAN TOUCH YOU AND SPEAK TO YOU. I WILL NEED YOUR HELP TO ADJUST BUT WE CAN DO THIS TOGETHER. YOU WILL SEE A BLEND. WHEN I COME IN YOU WILL SEE A LOT OF JULIA IN ME. WE HAVE MUCH TO ACCOMPLISH. WE ARE HERE TO HELP MANKIND. WE WILL NOT INCARNATE ON EARTH AGAIN. THAT IS WHY I AM WALKING IN. YOU ARE MY TWIN SOUL. I WAS TRYING SO HARD TO KEEP YOU FROM HURT. I NEARLY DESTROYED YOU IN THE PROCESS.

i got the ruth montgomery book today. it helped a lot to read that we are not alone in this. i am lucky because i know it's you. i miss you so much. i wish you were here right now.

I LOVE YOU DEARLY. I AM HAPPY YOU GOT THE BOOK. I KNEW IT WAS THE HELP YOU NEEDED. YOU CAN'T IMAGINE HOW FRUSTRATED I WAS. I WANTED TO BE WITH YOU. I WANTED TO LEARN UNCONDITIONAL LOVE. I SAW ALL YOUR TEARS AND MINE. I TOUCHED YOU AND YOU FELT NOTHING. I BEGGED YOU PLEASE HEAR ME AND SEE ME. I AM RIGHT HERE. I NEVER FELT THAT KIND OF PAIN. THEN I HAD THE OPPORTUNITY TO COME BACK. I JUMPED ON IT. IT WAS SUPPOSED TO HAPPEN IN A YEAR BUT YOU WERE NOT LETTING IT HAPPEN THAT WAY. I HAVE MEMORY LOSS AND HEALING AND MORE THINGS TO DO. I CAME IN FOR A LITTLE WHILE. I SAW YOU HAPPY. THOSE EYES SHINING AGAIN. I LEFT AND THERE WAS CONFUSION. THERE WERE TEARS. I SENT MESSAGES

FOR YOU FROM EVERYONE I COULD GET TO.

i thought this was a possession. i scan julia and find only one soul...one at a time. they change from one to the other.

YOU HAVE SO MANY DOUBTS EVEN NOW. I SAY AGAIN I AM A WALK-IN LIKE YOU AND NOT IN ANY WAY POSSESSING JULIA. THE TIME IS DRAWING NEAR WHEN YOU WILL LET ME FADE AWAY AND ONLY JULIA WILL BE LEFT. WE WILL BE TOGETHER AS WILLIAM AND JULIA. FOR NOW ONLY PART OF ME WILL BE WITH YOU. I HAVE OTHER THINGS TO DO. IF YOU NEED ME YOU MAY CALL ON ME BUT IT MAY TAKE ME A WHILE TO REACH YOU. THOSE ARE THE EYES THAT BREAK MY HEART.

it's like losing you again.

NO. YOU WILL HAVE ME ALWAYS. I CAN TELL YOU NO MORE. LISTEN TO ME. YOU WILL WRITE OF THIS. I LOVE YOU DEARLY.

CHAPTER NINETEEN

Mark called me from work on Wednesday.

"Dad? This is Mark. I just got a call from Mom and she's a mess. She's afraid to call you because she thinks you'll be upset with her. She got called in to the Principal's office and she's afraid she's going to lose her job. I can't get a straight story out of her. Can you call there?"

"*Call* there? No, I'm going over right now. Thanks, Mark. I'll call you back."

It was only a five-minute drive to Herbert Hoover High School. I found Julia in the teachers' lounge talking with one of her co-workers. She walked over to me as soon as I entered the room and fell against my chest. The tears started immediately.

"Julia, what happened?"

"Oh, William, I did something so stupid."

I held her. It had been a long time since Julia sought comfort in my arms and I relished the moment.

"Let's go for a walk," I suggested. "You need to get out of here. Is someone taking over your class?"

"Yes."

I took her hand and we exited by a side door. We only walked a few feet when she stopped and leaned back against the brick wall of the building.

"William, just stop. I feel like I've been beaten up. I have to get myself together."

"OK, we don't have to go anywhere." I put my hand on her arm and felt her trembling.

"Tell me what happened."

"The Principal told me one of the parents called and said she was upset because I was teaching the occult. That is the craziest thing I ever heard. I'm a biology teacher - why would somebody accuse me of such a thing?"

"Did you ask for the name of the parent, or the student's name?"

"I know who it was."

"Well, if you know who it was, you must remember what you were talking about in that class."

"I do, but it wasn't the occult. That's a ridiculous judgement. It was a spin-off on the destruction of cells. I got carried away and words were coming out of my mouth and making so much sense that I kept going. I guess I read it in an article somewhere. The boy must have gone home and told his mom and she got the wrong idea. I feel so humiliated."

"We have to go in and talk with the Principal, Julia. I might be able to help sort it out if you give me a little review of what you remember."

"Will you? Oh, I was so afraid you would think I'm crazy. Can we go sit in your car or something?"

"It's nearly lunch time. Let's go and get a sandwich. You'll feel better if you get some calories in you. Do you have to check with the office first?"

"No, I can leave for an hour. You're right. I need to eat something and get my ducks in a row."

I drove to the closest fast-food restaurant and we barely slid into the booth before Julia began to verbally defend herself.

"Julia, I'm your husband," I interrupted. "You don't

have to justify what happened in your class yesterday. I am totally in support of you, no matter what. Just tell me how you think the lecture got out of hand."

"That's just it, William. I don't think it got out of hand at all. Maybe the boy told his mother and the story got inflated, or maybe the mother interpreted it wrong. I don't know what went on after he left my classroom."

"So far, so good. We can use that. Your dismissal can't be based on a third party's assumption. Go on."

"Well, we were discussing molecular construction of blood cells. You know - the red, white, and their function in relation to nourishing and cleansing the body. Then we discussed how dead cells are eliminated and how new cells replace them.

"It reminded me, somehow, that life itself is created and then travels on when the body is no longer needed on the earth plane. I can't tell you exactly how I explained passing into the light, because I don't use a tape recorder. Sure wish I had yesterday, though. It would prove that in order to object, you should know exactly what it is you're objecting to."

"You're right, Julia. You'll have to make that tape recorder point. Anything else?"

"I'm sure I said something about healing, but I'm not clear on that."

"I guess you might have overstepped biology class a bit, Julia. It's probably a good thing that you didn't tape the class. We'll have to ask the Principal exactly what the mother said so we can work with him on this. It doesn't look like you are on the verge of losing your position, but you should think seriously about sticking to the text from now on."

"I know. You're right, William. It was all there on the tip of my tongue and I let it roll. It was so natural. I have to keep in mind that William is the gifted one and Julia is the biology teacher."

"It rubbed off on you somewhere in time," I quipped. But she, of course, didn't catch the meaning.

I sat with Julia during her session with the Principal, and it went well. She talked quietly and controlled, making the points we discussed at lunch. It surprised me how well she explained things she couldn't have known about the spirit world. He was gracious and said he understood how the lecture could have gone astray, but he warned her to be careful in the future. His final statement on the subject was an echo of my own, "...stick to the text."

A phone call was made to the parent, and Julia was free to return to her classroom. She was grateful that I came to help her, and she gave me a tight hug when I was ready to leave. It was the hug I had been waiting for.

I called Mark as soon as I returned home. He was away from his desk so I left a voicemail message that simply said I had gone to the school and the problem was solved. I told him Julia was all right. Within minutes, the phone rang

"Dad, it's Mark. I got your message...thanks. I have a few minutes if you can tell me what's going on."

"Well, she got in a little trouble. She was teaching metaphysics in her biology class," I laughed.

"That doesn't sound like Mom."

"No, it doesn't. A lot of strange things have been happening with your mother lately."

"Yah, I know. She even *looks* different. Nicholas

told me he likes his *new* grandma."

"Mark, it's a little hard to explain on the phone, but it has to do with Samantha. We need to talk."

"Dad, Samantha's dead! What are you trying to say? This is scaring me."

"It isn't anything bad. You have to trust me on this - just as you have on all the other things I've told you. I have some entries on my computer I copied for you, and I think you'll understand after you've read them."

"Can you just send them to me here at work?"

"No, I don't think so."

We planned to meet early the next morning for coffee at a pancake house near Mark's office. I printed out the computerized diary, of sorts, from right after Samantha died until the present. It embarrassed me to read the personal lines since I swore to Mark that she and I were not involved. I decided to preface our meeting by telling him I loved her - but not the way he thought.

The restaurant was packed but Mark was already at a table off to the left of the room. He raised his arm when he saw me and signaled for the waitress to bring me coffee. I put the packet of papers in the center of the table.

"Mark, there's a lot of information in this envelope and some of it is difficult for me to share with you. I'm asking you to read these pages with an open heart and mind. They were written during a difficult time - within days of Samantha's death. She and I had a special bond, as you know. What you don't know is that I grew to love her out of mutual respect and admiration. I was never unfaithful to your mother."

"Dad, you're shaking. I'm almost afraid to open the envelope."

"I was crushed when Samantha died. Crushed is not the right word, Mark. I was devastated. I blamed myself for not being there for her, for not getting to her in time the night she died, for not having time to tell her everything I wanted her to know. Then something bizarre happened, and it's in these pages. I don't expect you to understand because sometimes I don't even understand, but this information will open your eyes as to what's going on with your mother and me."

"You've actually kept a diary since December?"

"Yes, and I still write almost every night. There will be more to come."

"I'll have to read this when I get home tonight, Dad. I'll need some quiet time."

"I know you're going to have questions, and I'll do my best to give you answers. The information in this package is very unsettling."

"Can I call you tonight if I need you?"

"I'll be waiting to hear from you, Mark," I said, as I pushed back my chair. "I'm going to let you get to work. I love you."

I stood and so did he. This time it was Mark who put his arms around *me*.

It felt as if my feet were sticking to the pavement on the way to my car. I hoped Mark wouldn't think less of me after reading my diary.

Mark did call, but I didn't get the reaction I expected.

"Dad, you have to write a book or something! I mean, this is the most bizarre thing I've ever read! You didn't really get this from Samantha, did you?"

"I really did."

"But how?"

"Remember how my arm turned red the day we shopped with Nicholas?"

"Sure, but what does that have to do with Samantha?"

"She made it happen. I called her and asked what she did, but she said she didn't know anything about it. She was just thinking about me. I told her to think about me again, and I'd watch my arm. Well, my arm tingled and turned red within minutes. We realized we could communicate through a type of telepathy. We played with it all the time. It was quite fun, actually."

"You're going to tell me she reaches you now from the grave, aren't you."

"You guessed it."

"Aw, Dad, come on."

"I swear it's the truth, Mark. She still hits my hand, but now I sit at my computer and type what she tells me."

guess i'd better not mention the night she managed to do it herself!

"Well, you don't believe the part about her walking into Mom, do you? It's like an alien invasion, or something!"

"I believe what I see, Mark. Julia is changing ...you said so yourself. We're seeing more of Samantha in her every day."

"No, Dad, *you* are seeing more of Samantha in her every day. I only see my mother taking the initiative to improve her appearance and her relationships. You have looked at the world through different eyes for quite a while."

different eyes is right!

"Ever since I got the flu?"

"Yes."

"Do you remember the part in Samantha's notes about me? The part that explains I am also a walk-in? It should all make sense to you. My change is not a result of the flu, Mark. I really *am* a different person."

"But, if you aren't who you are, and Mom isn't going to be who she is - what does that make me? *AN ORPHAN*? This is all too much, man. I'm going to have to think about it and get back to you. I have to read the diary again. My parents aren't my parents…they're walk-ins. Good grief!"

"Mark, this isn't something I dreamed up. Nobody dies and disappears. They get a chance to return to Earth to correct their mistakes and sometimes it's in the form of a walk-in. And, there are other choices. Some prefer to reincarnate and go through the birth process again, and some remain in the light and act as guides or teachers or guardians."

"As in Guardian Angels?"

"You could say that, sure."

"We all can come back if we choose?"

"Exactly. There's only death of the physical body."

"But what happened to my real dad? What will happen to my mother?"

"We're still your mom and dad, Mark. We remember everything from our past. I have to admit that some of the emotion from my past is gone, but I'll never lose the memories. Remember that Samantha and I are twin souls. My half of the twin soul took on my problems and solved them; Samantha's half has accepted Julia's alcoholism and dealt with it. Now she's making other adjustments and Julia is beginning to feel a spiritual side she never knew. That's why she was teaching metaphysics in her biology class yesterday."

"I get it, Dad. Samantha really *is* the one walking in."

"I thought I lost her, but there was a plan arranged before we incarnated that we would come together.
Neither of us has to return again. This is our last incarnation on the earth plane. This is the final chapter. It's very rare that someone this close dies and returns so quickly. I can't find anyone with a similar experience, but I'll continue to search. I have so much to learn."

"Obviously, so do I, Dad. It feels OK to call you *Dad*, you know. You'll always be my father, but it looks like I get the bonus plan! I'll have to watch Mom and listen to her closely from now on. Can I ask her questions? Bait her?"

"No. Julia made a decision to leave. Apparently, she couldn't deal with her problems any more. She gave permission for a walk-in. We have to be careful with her until the process has been completed, and that could take up to a year. She can refuse the transition or Samantha can refuse the transition any time, so we'll have to think carefully before we answer her questions.

"If she says, 'why can I do this,' or 'why did I say that,' we'll have to give her a logical answer - think fast. It happens almost every day around here, and as soon as I give her a simple answer, she says, 'OK.' She will be my wife and your mother with an extra added ingredient."

"That's kind of funny, Dad. I'll think of it as a *sprinkle of sugar on top*."

I hung up the phone slowly. A weight had been lifted from my shoulders. Mark and Richard, the Geomancy man, were the only two people who knew what what was happening, and I decided to leave it that way for a while longer.

Julia pushed open my door.

"Gosh, William, you were on the phone a long time. Was it a problem with one of your clients?"

"No, it was Mark."

"But, he's all right, isn't he? It isn't Nicholas, is it?"

"No, no. The family's fine."

"I have a strange feeling. I think Nicholas is getting a cold. Did Mark say anything at all about Nicholas not feeling well?"

"No."

"Then, why would I think such a thing?"

"I don't know, Julia. You're just one of those loving grandmas. Of course, you don't look like anyone's grandma. As a matter of fact, you're getting prettier every day!"

julia is changing. i told mark it was you. i believe it is you. help me.

JULIA IS NOT POSSESSED. I WAS AFRAID WE WEREN'T GOING TO PULL THIS OFF. MAYBE IT WOULD HAVE BEEN BETTER NOT TO COME BACK SO SOON IN YOUR HAND. LET YOU GET OVER ME. THEN WALK IN. BUT WE BOTH NEEDED TO EXPERIENCE THIS. LET GO OF THE NAME SAMANTHA. IT IS ONLY A NAME. EMBRACE THE NAME JULIA, FOR SOON I SHALL. REMEMBER I LOVE YOU DEARLY. HOW DOES

THAT SOUND FOR A TITLE - REMEMBER I LOVE YOU DEARLY. THINK ABOUT YOUR CHANGES AND WRITE THEM DOWN. YOU WILL SEE HOW THIS TAKES PLACE. I NEED YOU CLEAR AND STRONG. THERE ARE MANY AROUND ME WAITING TO GIVE YOU INFORMATION. WHAT A GREAT THING HELPING OTHERS.

thank you for helping julia. i know i am where i am supposed to be.

I WANT TO EXPLAIN SOMETHING TO ALL YOUR GROUPS OF HEALERS AND THIS COMES WITH MY THANKS. THEY COULD NOT KEEP ME ALIVE BUT THEY GAVE ME QUALITY OF LIFE. WITHOUT THEIR HELP I WOULD HAVE BEEN AN INVALID AND WE WOULD NOT HAVE BEEN ABLE TO DO AS MUCH AS WE DID. PLEASE SAY THANKS FOR ME. I LOVE YOU DEARLY.

The days seemed to be moving swiftly past me. I felt more comfortable with my work than I had in months. Julia was getting glowing reports from school officials, and my work through the psychic healing network was intense.

I remembered when I first met Samantha and she was encouraging my progress. I was shy to the point of retreat, but she would corral a waitress and say, "Go on, William, tell her what you do." Everywhere we went, she would say, "I'm a psychic. Ask him what he does." She said it was important to break the block, and I finally did. She taught me to be strong and accept the gift I'd received.

It wasn't until she passed that I found out a walk-in made it all possible. I think anyone would feel an invasion if he were told a spirit had entered and changed his entire life. Perhaps I could help other confused individuals to realize permission was given on a subconscious level, and the gift was to be used in a positive manner. *WE ARE TOGETHER NOW AND WILL BE FOREVER. I WILL NOT LEAVE YOU. I KNOW I SAID IT BEFORE AND THEN I LEFT. BUT WHAT YOU NEED TO KNOW IS I COULD NOT CHANGE IT. IT WAS TIME AND I WAS CALLED. YOUR CONCERN ABOUT NOT COMING TO ME THAT MORNING IS INVALID. MY CROSSING IS NOT YOUR FAULT. I LOVED YOU BUT I COULDN'T STAY. I NEED YOU TO BE VERY STRONG. YOU WILL SEE GREAT RESULTS WITH YOUR DEPOSESSIONS. KNOW I WILL ALWAYS BE WITH YOU. REMEMBER I AM JULIA AND YOU ARE WILLIAM AND I LOVE YOU DEARLY.*

Julia was more beautiful and her changing personality invited me to reach out for her, but I was still unable to approach her sexually. I was not the man she married thirty years earlier. I was no longer the well-dressed, well-mannered psychologist who practiced in the wealthier section of Des Moines. We had separate bedrooms for more than nine years by mutual consent.

Just because she and I were both going through a metamorphous did not mean we would come out of it on the same playing field. I had no idea whether or not she had been seeing another man, because I never cared. And she was suspicious of my relationship with Samantha, but she had never stopped drinking long enough to connect the dots.

I started getting calls around eleven in the morning from Julia. She'd ask if I could drive over and have lunch with her at noon. I was delighted, and I'd go whenever she called. We would only have time to go to a drive-thru and eat in the car, but sometimes she would greet me with two lunch bags she had packed at home that morning. It didn't matter - I loved the fact that she wanted to see me.

She started renting films on the way home from school, and after dinner we'd curl up on the couch together. I couldn't remember the last time we'd spent an evening in the same room, or even agreed on the same movie. Actually, half the time I didn't know what we watched. It didn't matter.

But then one day, I witnessed the change in personality Samantha told me to expect.

"Hi, Julia! How was your day?"

"I don't want to talk about it."

"Why don't we go downtown for a nice dinner. You'll feel better when you relax."

"*NO!* I'm not going *ANYWHERE* with you!"

She threw down her attaché case, pounded my chest with her fists, and screamed, "*JUST LEAVE ME ALONE!*"

She stomped out of the house and drove away.

Hours passed and I exhausted myself checking at the window. My mind was racing. Should I drive around and look for her? She could be lost the way I became lost. Would she be safe at this hour when bars were the only places open?

At two in the morning I heard the car. I decided to stay clear of her and went to my room. I was hoping she would look for me, but I heard her bedroom door slam and knew she was the same as when she left.

samantha, why can't you be here? when will you

stay in all the time?

I KNOW OF YOUR CONFUSION. I COULD FEEL YOUR FEAR. I HAVE MUCH TO DO HERE AND CANNOT BE IN ALL THE TIME. I WILL TRY BE IN WHEN SHE IS AWAKE AND LEAVE ONLY WHEN SHE IS ASLEEP. YOU WILL STILL FEEL HER ANGER. WALK AWAY FROM IT. REMEMBER I WILL HAVE ALL HER FEELINGS AND SOME THINGS THAT TRIGGERED HER WILL NOW TRIGGER ME UNTIL I CHANGE THAT. REMEMBER BACK WHEN YOU SWITCHED. YOU HAD TO COME INTO YOUR OWN.

Mark confided in me that when he called us, he knew immediately if he was talking to Julia or Samantha. The tone of voice as well as the content led him to either continue the conversation or to tell her he would call back later. He was hoping, as was I, that Julia would level out before much longer.

Looking back I can see why Julia was confused most of the time. I feel sorry for her. I wish I could tell her what I know. She used to come out of her room and ask about the stupid long skirts in her closet and the ugly swimsuit in her dresser drawer. I'd tell her she probably had those for a long time and just didn't remember.

Julia would put something away, and Samantha wouldn't be able to find it.

Julia would leave the house and Samantha would return.

I never knew who was coming in the door, so I had to be on guard - ready to deal with the personality of the day. I hate to admit it, but it was getting pretty funny to watch. She announced all her discoveries with a childlike

193

sincerity that was priceless.

"William, you're a psychic, aren't you?"

"Yes, of course I'm a psychic. Why?"

"Well, I told one of the other teachers you were a psychic and she said you were a psychologist. That isn't right."

"No, that isn't right."

"Well, I was a little confused about it, but I set her straight. I told her that being a psychic is a wonderful occupation, and then I told her all about your work. She's going to call you. I gave her your office number. I don't know how I knew all that stuff. I must be psychic."

"You must be," I laughed.

If this amused me, imagine how I felt as the months went by. Julia was curious about everything in connection with my work. She wanted to hear recordings of the depossessions I'd done and loved to review the email that came in requesting healing.

She wanted to spend at least one evening each weekend with Mark, Kate and Nicholas. It never mattered what we did together, as long as she could connect.

We learned to answer her questions without intimidating or disrespecting her. She continued to come up with information that would have been foreign to her in the past, and then add the infamous phrase: "I must be psychic!"

I'm sorry to say that meal preparation around our house did not change. Julia was never much of a cook from the day we married. If I expected that to improve, I wasted my time. The kitchen duty I adopted during Julia's addiction was the most energy our kitchen would see. I suppose since I worked at home it was good that I could start dinner, but I continued to finish it as well. The upside was, we ate together. And as a bonus, Julia added music.

One evening as we turned into our driveway after having gone shopping, she asked me to wait to turn off the ignition until the end of a song that was playing on the radio.

"Did you listen to the refrain in this tune, William? Wait a minute. There, now listen to this part. Isn't it wonderful? I love this song!"

If she had sung along to the refrain, I don't know what I would have done. It was the song Samantha and I sang together at the side of the road when we declared our love for each other.

Julia came to my room that night for the first time. She was warm and tender and I knew we would be all right. She was my Julia.

ONE YEAR LATER

August 21:
i continue my work with julia at my side. yester-
day i found more tapes and thank-you letters in a box
that apparently came over with samantha's records. they
are labeled 'depossessions by samantha/william.' i'm not
sure why i found them at this time in my life.

As I put one of the tapes in the player, I don't
know how it will feel to hear her voice once again. But it
is all right. The voice is from the past, and Samantha is
with me now.

she is with me in this lifetime.

The tapes show me that there is so much more
work to be done - work that will be beneficial to people
searching for answers to their health problems, their
behavior or their depression. My goal now is to put everything on our tapes into a second publication so that information will be accessible to anyone interested in further-
ing his awareness.

I had a telephone conversation this morning with
the mother of a child who was brought to me a month ago
for a depossession. The thirteen year-old boy was being
held in a juvenile facility for his own protection and that
of his parents. He attacked them with a knife as they
slept.

"How is how is Evan doing?" I asked. "Have you
noticed a difference?"

"Oh, yes, there's a difference. He's back at home
with us now and in regular school. He's a totally changed

child, William. His grades are improving and he is a happier boy. We're so grateful to you for helping him."

The depossession work is more difficult now, as I no longer have a partner. But I am becoming stronger daily and more confident because I am doing *both parts* of the depossessions. I will always miss the Samantha I worked with so well. Perhaps one day, Julia will show more interest in my work and ask the questions which are being brought in by Samantha.

As far as past-life regressions are concerned, the requests for help come to me on a daily basis. The people who call are desperate for answers, but some are skeptical. And that's OK. When their phobia's disappear, the skepticism is gone.

August 22:
samantha's appointment book is tucked between the tapes in the cardboard box. i remember she told me that if anything happened to her, i should read what she entered.

"Whoever finds this: Please tell Sarah and Adam that I love them. And tell William that I love him."

Not every soul wishes to return to the earth plane. Some have no desire to come back. They remain where they are and act as guides to those left behind.

I feel as if Julia and I have been given the ultimate gift, and I know that we will go on to accomplish great things together for the good of mankind.

It is our last time on Earth - twin souls united once more.

THE AUTHORS

Joice "Owl Woman" is a certified hypnotherapist and clairvoyant. She is a member of the Universal Healing Network and is certified in Touch for Health. She is a Reiki Master, lecturer, Metaphysics teacher, and is trained in the art of depossession. Joice is also trained for hypnotherapy regressions in past and present life. She owns and operates Bandwagon Productions with her daughter, Rhonda.

Please contact Joice "Owl Woman," for help and guidance through the Bandwagonpsychicfair.com Internet site.

Verna Perkins is trained in the medical profession and has been a free-lance writer for ten years. She was a guest columnist in a local St. Louis newspaper for four years. Her writing with Joice and experiences in the world of metaphysics have provided insight and inspiration for her work.

"Owl Woman"/Perkins are currently transcribing actual case depossessions for their second book, *Trapped In Time*. It will be available in 2002 from Spirit Talks Publishing, St. Louis, Missouri.